Collins

English for Life

B2+ Upper Intermediate

Reading

Naomi Styles

Collins

HarperCollins Publishers
77-85 Fulham Palace Road
Hammersmith
London W6 8JB

First edition 2014

10 9 8 7 6 5 4 3 2 1

© HarperCollins Publishers 2014

ISBN 978-0-00-754231-4

Collins® is a registered trademark of HarperCollins Publishers Limited

www.collinselt.com

A catalogue record for this book is available from the British Library

Typeset in India by Aptara

Printed in China by South China Printing Co. Ltd

About the author

Naomi Styles trained as a Teacher of English as a Foreign Language in 1999, following a degree from the University of Wales and a varied set of jobs including agroforestry research, tour leading and working as a Christmas elf in Lapland! Since then, she has worked in Peru and the United Kingdom, teaching general, academic and business English to students of a wide range of level, ages and nationalities. She began work as a freelance writer of English language materials in 2009, and has since written a wide range of activities, courses and examination practice materials for both print and online publication.

CONTENTS

INTRODUCTION

Collins English for Life: Reading B2+ will provide you with the skills you need to read confidently in English.

Reading B2+ follows on from *Reading A2* and *Reading B1+* by practising and developing the skills taught at those levels. Readers can either work through the other books in the series before progressing to *Reading B2+*, or use this as a stand-alone book.

You can use *Reading B2+* in the classroom as supplementary material for a general English course, or it is also suitable for self-study.

Using Reading B2+

Reading B2+ consists of 20 units. Each unit focuses on a different function of communication via the written form. Like the other books in the series, *Reading B2+* includes a wide variety of text types. Many of these are authentic, that is, they are taken from real sources and remain unchanged. This allows readers to gain real insight into how vocabulary, style, tone and even grammar can change in different texts.

The book is divided into five sections:

Section 1 **Correspondence**   emails and instant messages, letters and invitations, written to specific individuals or to a wider audience, in varying tones

Section 2 **Products and service information**   everything related to the purchase and use of products and services in the modern world. Texts include labels, reviews, instructions and warranty information

Section 3 **Travel information**   from checking the travel and weather forecast and following a guided walk to reading a holiday itinerary and enjoying a travel blog

Section 4 **Factual information**   focusing on how facts and information are portrayed in different media. There are examples from newspapers, a textbook, an essay and a column. Particular attention is given to separating facts from conjecture, how emotive language can be used to enhance a text, and how texts and graphics can work together to present information.

Section 5 **Reading for pleasure**   short texts such as jokes and a poem, and excerpts from longer texts, both fictional and non-fictional, including a novel and an autobiography.

Unit structure

For ease of use, each unit follows a similar structure. It is recommended that you follow the order of exercises when working through a unit. Each unit follows the same pattern:

• A 'Getting started' section which presents questions for thought or discussion which will help you engage with the topic of the unit.

• Either one long text or a series of shorter texts related to the unit topic.

• Exercises to help you understand the general meaning of the text(s).

- Exercises focusing on details within the text.
- Exercises to help you identify and understand useful vocabulary within the text(s).
- Sometimes there will be a second text followed by further activities which expand upon the theme of the unit.
- Where relevant, a 'Reading tips' box gives you specific advice as to how to approach a text, and 'Language use' boxes point out interesting aspects of grammar used in the text(s).
- A 'Next steps' section suggests texts and activities you can do to further develop your skills in this topic area.

Reading skills and techniques

The reading skills developed in this book include skimming, scanning and reading for detail. The units introduce and practise useful vocabulary related to specific topics, and there are opportunities to practise:

- deducing meaning from context
- recognizing formal and informal vocabulary
- recognizing how word choice affects the tone of a text
- learning how phrasal verbs and idioms are used

Additionally, learners will gain insight into advanced reading techniques:

- understanding inference
- recognizing emotive and poetic language
- recognizing sarcasm and humour

Special attention is given to phrasal verbs and idioms. At the back of the book, there is a mini-dictionary which defines all of the phrasal verbs and idioms in the context in which they are used in this book. It also provides sentence examples which are taken from the Collins COBUILD Corpus.

Other features

At the back of the book, you will find the following useful sections. You may find it worthwhile to familiarize yourself with the appendices before you start working through the units.

- Four useful appendices providing guidance on the Common European Framework, reading strategies, study tips, common abbreviations and more.

- A Mini-dictionary of phrasal verbs and idioms gives definitions of the most useful phrasal verbs and idioms that are used in the reading passages throughout the units. Definitions are taken from the COBUILD Phrasal Verbs Dictionary and the COBUILD Idioms Dictionary.

Other titles

Also available in the *Collins English for Life* series at B2+ level: *Listening, Speaking* and *Writing*.

Available in the *Collins English for Life* series at A2+ and B1+ levels: *Reading, Listening, Speaking* and *Writing*.

1 INVITATIONS
Personal and public

Getting started

1 What was the last event you were invited to?

2 Who invited you? Was it a friend, family member or organization?

3 Think of three different ways you can receive an invitation.

A Social invitations

1 Read the invitations below and note down the following information:

the occasion	....	....
the venue	....	....
the time and date	....	....

1

> DAVID AND SOPHIA WEBSTER REQUEST THE HONOUR OF YOUR
> PRESENCE ON THE OCCASION OF THE MARRIAGE OF THEIR DAUGHTER
>
> ## *Louise*
> ### *to*
> ## *Sergio Martin*
>
> ON FRIDAY THE FOURTH OF JUNE AT TWELVE O'CLOCK
> WESTLAKE REGISTRY OFFICE
>
> TO BE FOLLOWED BY A RECEPTION AT:
> THE GEORGE COMMUNITY CENTRE, WESTLAKE. CARRIAGES AT MIDNIGHT
>
> R.S.V.P. BY THE THIRTY FIRST OF MARCH

2

TO	staff@brannigans.com
Subject:	Leaving do

Hi all,

As you may know, our intern Alba is returning to Spain, so we'd like to invite everyone in the department to a get-together on Friday to say farewell. We'll be in meeting room 4 from 5 p.m. onwards, and there'll be plenty of drinks and nibbles. Hope you can make it, even if only for a little while, so we can give her a good send-off! It would be good to know numbers, so please let me know if you can come.

Thanks!

Sameera
S. Rangoon
HR Manager

2 Read four replies. Are they responses to invitation 1 or invitation 2?

1 Many thanks for your kind invitation. I would be delighted to attend, and look forward to celebrating with you.   ....

2 Thanks for the invite! I've got a meeting at ten past but will pop in for a few minutes to say cheerio.   ....

3 I wouldn't miss it for the world. Will be such a shame to see her go. See you there!   ....

4 I regret that we will not be able to attend the ceremony due to a prior engagement. Please pass on our congratulations.   ....

Language note

It is important to be able to recognize whether an invitation is formal or informal so that you can respond appropriately.

Formal invitations use formal verbs (*request*) and are more likely to use sentences than questions.

Informal invitations may drop the subject of the sentence, and may use phrasal verbs (*pop in*), idioms (*I wouldn't miss it for the world*), phrasal nouns (*get-together*) and exclamation marks (*!*).

3 Complete gaps a–f with formal or informal phrases from exercises 1 and 2.

Formal	Informal
a	*We would like to invite you to ...*
R.S.V.P.	**b** ....
c	*I can't make it.*
Many thanks for your kind invitation.	**d** ....
I would be delighted to attend.	**e** ....
f	*something on*

4 Consider whether each sentence is formal or informal. Then circle the most appropriate word or phrase to complete the sentences.

1 You are cordially invited to attend a *reception / get-together* to welcome our visitors from China.

2 Won't be able to make Carla's leaving *event / do* on Thursday – sorry. I've got *a prior engagement / something on*.

3 Cheers for the invite. *I would be delighted to attend / Would love to come*.

4 *It is with deepest regret that / Ever so sorry but* we are obliged to *turn down / decline* your kind invitation.

http://www.inspiredbypeople.org/charity-events

inspired
by people

Transparent, Passionate, Sustainable

| Home | About | Events | Fundraising | Donate | Contact us |

Fundraising events - together we can make a difference

Dear Friends,

We can't believe how quickly the last two years have flown by! It all began with the idea to support the most vulnerable people in developing countries by linking with local NGOs that have a similar vision: to reach out to the poorest communities and make a BIG difference! After lots of paper work, discussions, meetings with sponsors, and communication with our overseas selected projects, we managed to establish this wonderful charity. With the support of our donors, volunteers, friends and sponsors over the past two years, we have been able to help our partnering organizations in raising awareness and offering financial support for their projects in Nepal, India and Malawi. *Inspired by People* works with small grass roots projects that make a difference, including a trauma recovery centre in Nepal. We will soon be building a school in Malawi.

We have had a wonderful and fulfilling first couple of years and on Saturday 12 Nov, you & and your friends are invited to celebrate IBP's 2nd Anniversary!

Our mission is to support sustainable and existing projects that help the most vulnerable people. We do this with 100% giving, so after the cost of the venue and the refreshments, whatever we receive will go to our projects!

By coming to our events you are already supporting our projects but there is always an opportunity to do more... you can leave us a donation or get involved as a volunteer ... feel free to talk to us during the evening.

We have reserved a private room @ Valmont Club until 11 p.m. and afterwards a large seating area. All our guests will be offered a complementary soft drink and nibbles on arrival to get the night started and 20% discount on soft drinks until 10.30 p.m.

Cost: £25 - please follow link and make payment: you will be placed on the guest list :) Don't forget to invite your friends!
Get your tickets here. Tickets are limited, so it is advisable to book in advance.

Please arrive between 9-10.30 p.m. for a complementary entry; otherwise the cover charge would be £10 each until 11.30 p.m. and £15 thereafter.

Dress code: smart casual.

If you are unable to come and congratulate us, but are still willing to show your support for our hard work, please feel free to make a DONATION here.

To be on our guest list, you need to "LIKE" our facebook page AND to be shown as "Attending" on our event page.

We also accept donations by text: Text IBP10 to send £10 (or whatever amount you would like to donate) to 70070. This is sponsored by Vodafone and 100% will go directly to our overseas projects.

We look forward to welcoming you and celebrating together!

Best,
IBP Team
Valmont Club

B   An invitation to a charity event

1 Read the invitation on the opposite page. Is it written in a formal or informal style? Note the elements that helped you decide.

2 Scan the invitation and note down the main details.

1 Reason for celebration ....

2 Date   ....

3 Location   ....

4 Start time   ....

5 Entry cost ....

6 Dress   ....

3 Read the invitation and complete the sentences.

1 *Inspired by People* is a ....

2 IBP's work includes a project at a .... and they will soon be building a school.

3 100% of proceeds, after the cost of the .... and ...., will go towards their projects.

4 You are invited to discuss .... or .... with the IBP team during the evening.

5 The event will be popular, so you must ....

6 The total entry cost if arriving at 11 p.m. will be ....

7 On arrival, you will receive a .... and nibbles.

8 You'll also receive a .... on soft drinks until 10.30 p.m.

9 To get on the guest list, you must .... the Facebook page and show that you are attending the event.

10 You can make donations to the charity by texting .... to ....

4 Match the vocabulary from the text to the definitions below.

1	sponsors	a	money given to support a charity
2	grass-roots	b	additional fee
3	mission	c	free
4	complementary	d	aim or goal
5	cover charge	e	people or organizations who give money
6	donations	f	ordinary people at the most basic level

Next steps

Visit the following websites and find out what social events they are holding soon. Make a list of possible events to attend with the dates and costs of the events.

www.cancerresearchuk.org

www.oxfam.org.uk

2 REQUESTS AT WORK
Memos, emails and formal letters

Getting started

1 What sort of requests do you receive in your daily life?
2 What sort of requests do clients receive from businesses?
3 In what situations do you receive written requests?

A   Everyday requests

1 Skim through the four requests to Helen Draper, assistant manager at Stevens Electrical Ltd. For each request identify what the writer wants.

1

> Stevens Electrical.
> 9447, 47 Ave.
> Albuquerque, NM
>
> 10047, W.22 St.
> Albuquerque, NM
> 11 July 2013
>
> Dear Sir / Madam,
>
> Our records indicate that you have an outstanding balance of $543.89 with a due date of the 8th July. We have yet to receive this payment. Please find a copy of the invoice enclosed.
>
> If this amount has already been paid and sent, please disregard this notice and we apologize for any inconvenience. Otherwise, please forward us the amount stated above. As our written agreement states, we will start charging a 5% interest on any outstanding balance after 15 days.
>
> Thank you for your cooperation regarding this matter. We sincerely hope we can continue doing business together in the future.
>
> Sincerely,
> J. Hunt
> Accounts Manager

2

> Helen,
> Please can you pick up some stamps when you go out later? We need some ASAP. Use the petty cash – and don't forget to get a receipt. Thanks!
> Rachel

3

> TO   Admin@stevenselectrical.com
> Subject: Alarm System estimate
>
> To whom it may concern
>
> I am writing to request an estimate for an alarm system for our new headquarters which will be located in Springfield, Kansas. Enclosed is a package which outlines the specifications for our request and the layout of the buildings. Please submit your signed and sealed bid by 5 p.m. on August 1, along with a guarantee that you can finish the system within two weeks of signing the contract.
>
> Thank you for your kind consideration,
>
> H. Hodge
> Greenfield Ltd.

4

> TO   hdraper@stevenselectrical.com
> Subject: Leaving Early
>
> Dear Helen,
>
> Would it be possible for me to leave early on Thursday afternoon as I have a dental appointment? Ideally, I need to leave by 3 p.m. at the latest. I assure you that I will complete all urgent work beforehand, and can make up the hours on Friday. I'd appreciate it if you could let me know if this is acceptable by the end of the day, so that I have ample time to rearrange the appointment if necessary.
>
> Thanks,
> Jenny

2 Complete the sentences with the correct answer.

1   The payment in letter 1 is …

    a   overdue.   **b**   due in 15 days.

2   Rachel's request is …

    a   urgent.   **b**   not urgent.

3   Request 3 is from a …

    a   current client.   **b**   potential client.

4   Jenny is probably Helen's …

    a   line manager.   **b**   assistant.

Reading tip

Make sure you scan the whole text when making notes. Don't stop reading after you've located the information you're looking for. There may be more information later on, and you might miss something important.

3 Complete the table with the tasks that Helen must do in order of priority, starting with the earliest deadline.

Priority	Task	Deadline
1		
2		
3		
4		

4 Find words with the meanings below. The number of the text it appears in is given.

1 an amount of money that you owe (2 words, request 1)

2 a document listing work done and its cost (request 1)

3 extra money charged for borrowing money (request 1)

4 money kept in the office to buy small items (2 words, request 2)

5 a guess at how much something will cost (request 3)

6 an offer to do work for a particular amount of money when other people are competing to do the same work (request 3)

7 a legal document stating the terms and conditions of an agreement (request 3)

8 plenty of (request 4)

Language note

The type of language used when making requests reflects the social position of the sender and recipient, the level of formality and the nature of the request.

A formal request may use 'Please' and the infinitive form.

Please forward us the amount stated above.

Simple requests to people you know well often use 'Can'.

Can you pick up some stamps when you go out later?

Requests for permission or favours often use more polite phrases.

Would it be possible for me to leave early on Thursday afternoon?

I'd appreciate it if you could let me know by the end of the day.

5 Look again at the four requests.

1 Circle the phrases used to make formal requests.

2 Underline the phrase used to make an informal request.

3 Which requests are more formal? Those from strangers / those from people you know?

4 Which requests are more formal? Those from your employees / those from your manager?

5 Is it always necessary to use 'please' when making polite requests? Yes / no

... each gap.

	appreciate	**c**	welcome	**d**	realize
	delete	**c**	forget	**d**	cancel
	recognize	**c**	accept	**d**	take
	submitted	**c**	proposed	**d**	presented
	probable	**c**	possible	**d**	preferable
	atest	**c**	least	**d**	last
	necessities	**c**	commands	**d**	requirements
	onviction	**c**	association	**d**	relief

...negie Hotel

... Ave. Albuquerque, NM

... nquiry about booking a function room for the evening

... dered whether you still intended to make this booking.
... pay the deposit within the next five days. If you have recently
... this part of the letter and **3** .... my apologies.

... tional services we offer, including refreshments and
... e services, would it be **5** .... for you to let
... .? This will give us ample time to prepare the
... .

... garding this matter.

www.writeexpress.com and note down different ways of making

3 ONLINE FORUMS
Looking for advice

Getting started

1 Where do you go to for advice?

2 Would you prefer to speak to somebody or go online?

3 Why do you think people choose to get advice from online forums?

A Asking for advice

1 Read the post on the website, then answer the questions below.

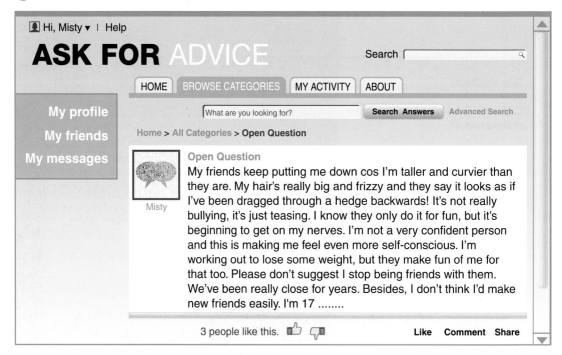

Hi, Misty ▼ | Help

ASK FOR ADVICE

Search [   ]

HOME | BROWSE CATEGORIES | MY ACTIVITY | ABOUT

My profile
My friends
My messages

[What are you looking for?]   **Search Answers**   Advanced Search

Home > All Categories > **Open Question**

Open Question

Misty

My friends keep putting me down cos I'm taller and curvier than they are. My hair's really big and frizzy and they say it looks as if I've been dragged through a hedge backwards! It's not really bullying, it's just teasing. I know they only do it for fun, but it's beginning to get on my nerves. I'm not a very confident person and this is making me feel even more self-conscious. I'm working out to lose some weight, but they make fun of me for that too. Please don't suggest I stop being friends with them. We've been really close for years. Besides, I don't think I'd make new friends easily. I'm 17 ....

3 people like this. 👍 👎   Like   Comment   Share

1 Which title is best for Misty's post?

  a   How can I meet new friends?

  b   What should I do about my so-called friends?

  c   Can anyone give me fashion advice – fast?

2 Which discussion category would you expect to find this question in?

  a   Fun > Meet new people

  b   Health > Women's Health

  c   Family & Relationships > Friends

3   Which abbreviation best fits in the final gap?

    a   BRB   **b**   IMHO   **c**   BTW

2   **Answer the questions.**

    1   How does Misty describe her appearance and personality?

    2   What does Misty mean by 'My friends keep putting me down'? How do they do this?

    3   How does Misty feel about her friends' behaviour?

B   Giving advice

1   **Read the advice from other website users. Complete gaps 1–6 in the website with the following sentences.**

    a   If I were you, I wouldn't make a big deal of it.

    b   Real friends don't go out of their way to upset you.

    c   See how they like it.

    d   If they really are your friends, they'll understand and stop.

    e   In a few years time I bet you'll be gorgeous, believe you me.

    f   Just make sure you are doing it for yourself and not because your friends are pushing you into it.

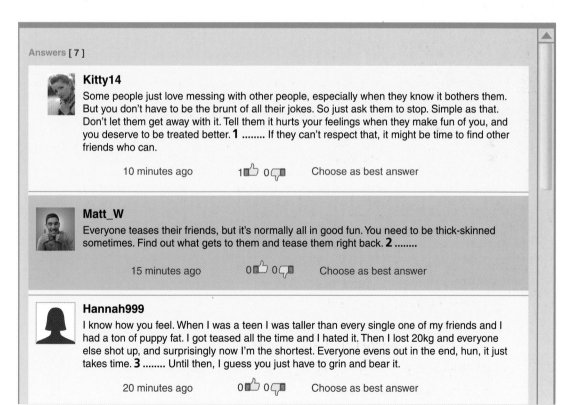

Answers [7]

Kitty14

Some people just love messing with other people, especially when they know it bothers them. But you don't have to be the brunt of all their jokes. So just ask them to stop. Simple as that. Don't let them get away with it. Tell them it hurts your feelings when they make fun of you, and you deserve to be treated better. **1** .... If they can't respect that, it might be time to find other friends who can.

10 minutes ago   1 👍 0 👎   Choose as best answer

Matt_W

Everyone teases their friends, but it's normally all in good fun. You need to be thick-skinned sometimes. Find out what gets to them and tease them right back. **2** ....

15 minutes ago   0 👍 0 👎   Choose as best answer

Hannah999

I know how you feel. When I was a teen I was taller than every single one of my friends and I had a ton of puppy fat. I got teased all the time and I hated it. Then I lost 20kg and everyone else shot up, and surprisingly now I'm the shortest. Everyone evens out in the end, hun, it just takes time. **3** .... Until then, I guess you just have to grin and bear it.

20 minutes ago   0 👍 0 👎   Choose as best answer

Sergio_82

Stop hanging out with them. You can do better.

22 minutes ago   0 👍 1 👎   Choose as best answer

SportFan

First off, congrats on trying to lose weight. **4** .... I would advise you to take up karate or join a fitness class or something. You will probably meet some nicer people while you're there.

45 minutes ago   2 👍 1 👎   Choose as best answer

Thomas_B

I get teased all the time 'cos I'm shorter than everyone else. **5** .... Just laugh along. Tell them 'Watch it, 'cos I'm bigger than you', or tell them they're vertically challenged. It's not worth losing friends over.

1 hour ago   0 👍 0 👎   Choose as best answer

SuperGirl

Dumping friends isn't easy especially when you haven't got anyone else to turn to, so I understand why you wouldn't want to find new friends. I suggest talking to each of your friends individually and telling them that you don't appreciate their comments, especially when you are making an effort to slim down. They might not have realized how much you took it to heart. If that doesn't work, you need to distance yourself from them. **6** ....

1 hour ago   1 👍 0 👎   Choose as best answer

2 Match the advice on the website to summaries 1–6. Write the name of the person who gives the advice.

1 It won't last forever.   ....
2 Joke about it.   ....
3 Find new friends.   ....
4 Tell your friends how you feel (x2). ....
5 Get a new hobby.   ....
6 Tease your friends back.   ....

Reading tip

When reading informal advice, think about the writers' attitudes to help you decide which advice to trust.

- Is the poster sincere and sympathetic or joking and uncaring? A sympathetic person will consider another person's feelings. An uncaring person might disregard feelings, or ignore parts of the question.
- How much effort has the person put into their response? Longer texts may indicate greater effort has been put in.
- Is the advice worth following? Someone who uses their own experience to illustrate their answer may be able to give a more valid response.

3 Read the Reading tip. Then answer the questions.

  1 Which posters are sympathetic to Misty? Underline the phrases which show sympathy.

  2 Which posters are least sympathetic? What makes you think this?

  3 Which advice do you think Misty should follow?

4 Underline the phrases used to give advice in the responses. Use them to complete the following posts.

  1 If .... would find some new friends. (4 words)

  2 I would .... to get a make-over, so you feel more confident about yourself. (2 words)

  3 I .... developing a hobby, so you can meet people who appreciate you for what you are, not what you look like. (1 word)

  4 It might .... find a new set of friends. (3 words)

5 What do the following phrases mean?

  1 the brunt of all their jokes (Kitty14)

     a someone who makes a lot of jokes   **b** someone who people laugh at

  2 thick-skinned (Matt_W)

     a sensitive and understanding   **b** emotionally strong

  3 vertically challenged (Thomas_B)

     a someone who is shorter than average   **b** someone who is taller than average

6 Complete the advice below with phrasal verbs or expressions from the box. Change the part in bold where necessary.

go out of **someone's** way	take **something** to heart	turn to
make a big deal out of **something**	distance **oneself** from	grin and bear it

  1 If you're feeling down, you can always .... good friends and family.

  2 I'd advise you to stop .... to please him. He doesn't deserve it.

  3 It sounds as though your sister was only joking. You shouldn't ....!

  4 You always .... things. Try to calm down!

  5 If your friend's behaviour is embarrassing you so much, I suggest you .... her.

  6 If you hate your job, you need to decide whether to quit or ....

Next steps

Go to an online advice forum and make a note of the phrases used to give advice.

Think of a problem or issue in your own life. Use the search function on the online forum to find posts from people who have asked for similar advice. Can you find your answer?

4 SHARING NEWS
Short updates and longer letters

Getting started

1 Do you sometimes send letters and cards in the post?
2 How do your friends update you about their latest activities?
3 Do you keep in contact with people you rarely see?

A   Instant messages

1 Match the messages with the life events.

1 I hear Tim finally popped the question. Glad to hear she said yes!

2 Guess what! Alicia is eating for two!

3 Li passed her exams with flying colours.

4 Did you hear? Bruno passed away last Sunday – but at 103, he certainly had a good innings!

5 Everything's strangely quiet here now the kids have flown the nest.

6 It's Jian's last day in the office. He's decided to go it alone.

7 Did you know Ricardo and Anna tied the knot last week? They had a beach ceremony in Hawaii.

8 Here's a pic of our bundle of joy – Alex. Arrived early on Tuesday morning ... 3.2kg.

a pregnancy
b leaving home
c birth
d graduation
e starting a business
f death
g marriage
h engagement

2 Match the replies below to the announcements above.

a About time too! Have they set a date yet? ...1...

b Really? I didn't even know they were getting married. ....

c Oh wow! When's it due? ....

d Try and look on the bright side – no more ferrying them around! ....

e All credit to her! She certainly put the work in. I bet she's delighted! ....

f Super news! You must be so proud. ....

g Sorry to hear that. I'll send my condolences to Margaret. ....

h Well I hope it works out for him. ....

Language note

If you come across a confusing phrase in an informal text, it may be an idiom. Word-for-word, idioms don't make sense. But by looking at the idiom as a chunk of language, it is often possible to guess its meaning from the context. The words and word order of an idiom are fixed, meaning that you cannot usually change the order or replace one of the words with a synonym. Examples include 'tie the knot' = get married or 'bundle of joy' = a baby.

3 Complete the idioms. Then write the order in which these events usually take place in a person's lifetime.

1 to propose marriage = ... the ....

2 to be pregnant = ... for ....

3 to pass with distinction = pass with ....

4 to have a long life = have a ....

5 to leave home = fly the ....

6 to get married = tie the ....

7 to have a baby = have a .... of joy ....

8 to regularly give someone a lift = ... someone around ....

4 The idioms in the instant messages below have been used incorrectly. Correct them.

Becky:
Guess what! Simon popped a question to Julia while they were on holiday.

....

Laura:
Jenny told me she was eating with two. It's due in December.

....

Li Yao:
I passed my driving test with a flying colour! Am totally over the moon!

....

Martin:
I went to see Helen and Mark's new joy bundle last Saturday – she's gorgeous!

....

5 Complete the email below with phrasal verbs and idioms from Exercises 1 and 2. Change the form of the verbs where necessary.

Hi Jade,

Sorry it's been ages since I wrote. I've had such a lot on my plate since I decided to quit my job at the firm and 1 .... as a contractor. Of course, I'm over the moon that's it's all 2 .... so well for me, but I seem to be constantly up to my ears in work. I thought that once the kids had 3 .... I'd have time on my hands, but so much for that! I'm busy preparing for Lucy's wedding – did you know that she's 4 .... next month? Her boyfriend 5 .... two months ago while they were on holiday in New York. I'm also looking after Caroline's 6 .... twice a week, which is hard work, and Caroline's 7 .... again – this one's due in November. I think it was easier when they were both living at home and all I had to do was 8 .... !

Anyway, that's all my news. Hope all's well with you and yours!

Best wishes
Eve

B   Personal letters

1   Read the letter on page 23. Write names for the people in the family tree below.

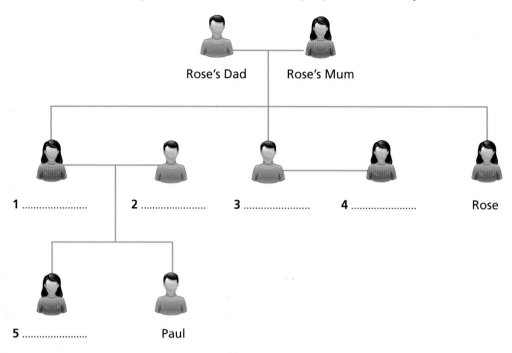

Rose's Dad   Rose's Mum

1 ....   2 ....   3 ....   4 ....   Rose

5 ....   Paul

2   Tick the events that are mentioned in Rose's letter.

birth	....	a house move	....
leaving school	....	pregnancy	....
graduation	....	leaving home	....
marriage	....	illness	....
a new job	....	retirement	....
engagement	....	death	....

3   Read the sentences and put a tick in the correct column.

	True	False	No information
1 There were over 100 guests at Simon's wedding.	....	....	....
2 Rose is in her second year at university.	....	....	....
3 Rose quit the hockey team.	....	....	....
4 Rose will stay at her cousin's house in Dubai.	....	....	....
5 Hannah brought her baby to the wedding.	....	....	....
6 Both Rose's nan and granddad are in poor health.	....	....	....

12 Mounts Lane
Hanchurch
30th December

Dear Sofia,

I can't believe another year has flown by! I thought I'd write and let you know what we've all been up to.

The most exciting event was my brother Simon's wedding in August. It was a traditional wedding in the English countryside – and with English weather, unfortunately. Dark clouds and drizzle all day, but we did manage to get all the photos taken outdoors, and we thoroughly enjoyed ourselves. Rebecca also invited mum and yours truly to her hen do a couple of weeks before the big day, which was a spa and pampering weekend. It was lush!

It's been an eventful year for me too. So far, the second year at uni has been considerably tougher than the first. I've had so much coursework that I had to pull a few all-nighters. I even considered bowing out of the hockey team because of all the pressure, but friends persuaded me to keep at it, and I'm glad they did, because it does give me a welcome break from the library!

I decided to take up the opportunity of a year's work placement before my final year. It was hard to find one, though. Placements got snapped up really quickly, and for a while I thought I wouldn't find anything. Thankfully, my cousin Rob helped me get an internship at the bank where he works in Dubai. It ticks all the boxes – a big company, an exciting city, decent pay, so I'm hoping it'll pan out well.

I'm hoping to get to France in the New Year, so I can catch up with my sister and her family there. She had another baby in June – a boy this time, Paul. They all came over for the wedding of course, but they couldn't stay long because Duncan had to get back to work. Hannah's in her element. Kirstin is enjoying having a little brother to play with. They're really settled in Marseilles now – they love the city and I can't see them ever moving back. I'm also planning to pop in on my nan and granddad over the holiday. Nan's not in the best of health and looking after her is taking its toll on granddad. He still hangs on to his classic car, although he does find driving a lot more stressful than he used to.

Anyway, I think that's all from me. Here's wishing you a great holiday and all the best for the New Year. Do get in touch.
With much love,
Rose

4 Choose the correct meaning for phrases 1–6.

1 yours truly

    a to you   **b** from me

2 pull an all-nighter

    a study all night   **b** sleep all night

3 ticks all the boxes

    a is a good choice for many reasons   **b** takes a lot of effort

4 is in her element

    a is happy doing something she likes   **b** is struggling

5 taking its toll

    a making life easier   **b** making life more difficult

6 days ... may be numbered

    a it may happen soon   **b** it may end soon

5 Complete the sentences below with phrasal verbs from the text. The first letter and number of words is given.

1 I'm having such a great time at uni – the term seems to have f............. ....

2 I wasn't enjoying being team captain, so I decided to b............. ....

3 I'm fed up with applying for jobs, but I know if I k............. ...., I'll find my dream job soon.

4 I s............. .... my uncle's offer of a holiday in Greece.

5 I'm starting an internship next month. I'll let you know how it p ....

6 I hope to p............. .... on David and his family while I'm in Italy.

6 Rose's friend sends the reply on the opposite page. Read sentences a and b and decide which is best.

Language note

Do, does and *did* can be used before present or past simple positive verbs. They are used for emphasis, and are used more in personal than formal writing.

They can emphasize a contrast between this and the preceding statement or sentence, or a strong like or dislike.

---

7 Highlight all uses of emphatic *do, does* or *did* in both Rose's letter and Sofia's reply. In each case, identify its function.

Dear Rose,

Thank you so much for sending me the news about your family. What a busy year you've had! I'm so pleased to hear that Simon has got married.

1 a I'm glad you were lucky with the weather on the big day!
   b What a shame about the weather. Never mind, I'm sure you made the best of it.

The spa day sounds like a lot of fun. It's a shame your sister didn't go too.

2 a I expect she was too busy with the new baby.
   b But it's a long way for a pregnant woman to travel.

It sounds as though she and her family love where they live.

3 a She must be pretty good at the language by now.
   b She always did love being in the countryside.

I'm really glad you managed to find a work placement.

4 a You're going to love living in London.
   b It was nice of your cousin to put a word in for you.

It sounds to me as if...

5 a you're really enjoying university.
   b your studies are getting you down a bit.

Just make sure you do enjoy yourself too!

6 a Relax and enjoy your time with your sister and family when you go to Dubai.
   b Relax and enjoy your time with the family in France.

I'm sorry to hear...

7 a about your nan, but as they say, she had a good innings!
   b that your nan is not doing too well, but I'm sure she's in good hands with your granddad.

Give them my love when you see them.

8 a I'm so glad that he hasn't got rid of that lovely car yet.
   b What a pity he no longer has that wonderful old car.

I did love it when he took me out for a spin in it!
On that note, I think it's time for me to sign off.
Thank you again for your letter.

Love,
Sofia

Next steps

Search for 'The Cat that could open the fridge' on an online bookstore such as Amazon. What is this book about? Read the reviews.

5 ADVERTS
Services and special offers

Getting started

1 Which shops and services do you use in your neighbourhood?
2 Where is the best place for local businesses to advertise their services?
3 What special offers might shops and services have to attract customers?

A Classified ads

1 Complete the classified ads with the type of service from the box. You will not need them all.

beauty salon	mobile phone unlocking	health club
driving school	computer repairs	tuition

1

Advance Now a ....

Est. 1985
Beginners – Learners with disabilities – Refresher courses
Male and female instructors

Fully qualified instructors – NO TRAINEES GUARANTEED!
Wide choice of vehicles to choose from – manual and automatic
Extensive library of books and CD-Roms available free of charge to help you prepare for your theory test

Discounts on block bookings
2 for 1 offer on your first lessons
We have the highest pass rate in the local area
You can't afford to learn anywhere else!

Call 0800 577 3668 now!

2

The Right Place
Running Slow?
Need an upgrade?

Call 01288 347299 For all your **b** ....
Huge range of services:
Virus removal, data recovery, troubleshooting, software and hardware installation, screen replacement, maintenance and support and much more

competitive prices – free 24/7 call-out service – free no obligation quotes – no charge for collection or delivery – no fix, no fee

10% off services with the production of this ad

3

Education
Solutions

- One-to-one and small group c .... (10 max.)
- Range of subjects – Maths, English, Sciences and Humanities
- All levels, including university entrance
- Short and long courses
- Dyslexia Support

OUR PROMISE

We strive to enable all children and young adults to unlock their potential. All our staff have undergone rigorous quality checks to ensure that you succeed.

Easy-to-reach central London location ● Daytime, eves. and weekends ● Affordable Prices

Call us to book your free trial!

4

🏃 New You d ....

Best value facilities and service in town!

Over 80 aerobic and fitness classes per week in 5 state-of-the-art studios
Top class equipment to suit all goals and abilities
Personal training and weight loss guidance

Book now for a free personal induction!
One of our friendly instructors will create an individual workout plan especially designed for you to meet your goals.

Sauna - Crèche - Free parking

Pay per month membership, no annual contract necessary
existing members: refer a friend and get one month free (terms and conditions apply)
Discounts for OAPS and off-peak members

You're more than just a member

2   Which service 1–4 in Exercise 1 ...

1   offers a cheaper rate for the elderly? ....

2   will not charge customers if the service is unsuccessful? ....

3   allows people to sample their service without paying? ....

4   will provide two services for the cost of one? ....

5   gives readers a money-off voucher? ....

6   will estimate the cost without expecting you to use their service? ....

3 Read the sentences and put a tick in the correct column.

	True	False	No information
1 *Advance Now* uses trainee instructors to teach driving students.	....	....	....
2 You can buy books and CD-Roms from *Advance Now*.	....	....	....
3 You can phone *The Right Place* in the middle of the night.	....	....	....
4 All tutors at *Education Solutions* have university qualifications.	....	....	....
5 To study with *Education Solutions*, you must book a minimum of 10 lessons.	....	....	....
6 *New You's* free health appraisal helps people decide whether to become members.	....	....	....
7 Membership at *New You* is cheaper if you go at certain times of day.	....	....	....

4 Choose the correct word to complete the adverts.

1 Professional cleaning at *complimentary / affordable* prices.

2 *Call out / Refer* a friend and get a 20% discount on your next order.

3 T J Simpsons Electricals. No job too small. Call us now for a no *discount / obligation* quotation.

4 Washing machine repairs. Same day service. No *call-out / off-peak* charges.

5 Rui Karate – 6 years plus and adults. Call to arrange a free *trial / block* lesson.

6 The Ink Man – printer and photocopier inks. Lowest prices *guaranteed / afforded*.

7 Squash and tennis courts available. 15% discount on all block *bookings / memberships*.

8 13 months' membership for the price of 12. Terms and conditions *exist / apply*.

B Special offers

1 Read about some of the special offers available at *New You*. Which offer would suit the following customers?

1 Agnieska is 69 years old and only plans to go to the gym in the early afternoon.

2 Cathy is only interested in joining a health club to attend aerobics classes.

3 Omar wants to play football with some colleagues on a regular basis.

4 Claudia is already a member, and is trying to convince her sister to join too.

2 Use the text to answer *yes* or *no* to the following customer queries.

1 Is it true that I can use the gym for six months for only £10 if I sign up this month?

2 So, unless I'm a member, I have to pay £5 per fitness class. Is that right?

3 Can I take advantage of the Manager's Special to make a regular booking on Thursdays?

4 Can Silver Fitness members who sign up for a year get a month's free membership?

5 Can I bring a friend to a 1 hour exercise class every week for a month free of charge?

6 I've got Social You membership. Do I still have to pay each time I attend a fitness class?

| Home | Facilities | OFFERS | How to find us | Contact |

Fitness Special

To celebrate the opening of our new fitness suite, get 3 month's membership for just £10 when you sign up for a minimum of 6 months, but be quick – this offer is only valid THIS MONTH. This amazing deal gives you free access to the gym, pool and sauna between 7 a.m. and 10 p.m., and access to our fitness classes at just £1 per session (standard non-member fee £5). Don't miss out – sign up today!

Manager's Offer

Want to get together for a weekly kickabout? Then check out our Manager's Offer – 25% off our 3G astro pitch when you block book a minimum of 10 weekend slots – that's a saving of up to £87.90!

Regular's Offer

Make a long term commitment to your health and fitness and get one month's all-inclusive membership free when you take out a year's membership with us. That's a saving of up to £49.70! And yes, this can be used in conjunction with our other fantastic deals.

Silver Fitness

Over 60? Shape up with full access to the pool, gym, fitness classes and sauna (between 10 a.m. and 4 p.m.) for just 60% of the standard adult membership fee.

Buddy Pass

Have fun with your friends! The Buddy Pass lets you bring along a friend once a month for a 3 hour session completely free of charge. If your friend then signs up, you'll get a month's membership absolutely free! Terms and conditions apply.

Social You

Enjoy working out with others? For a one-off annual fee of £50, choose from our wide range of fun classes for just £1 per session. This offer does not entitle you to use the gym, pool or sauna.

Next steps

Use a classified ads website such as *Craigslist* or *Gumtree* to find details of

- a health club in New York, USA
- a computer repair service in Liverpool, UK
- a driving school in Melbourne, Australia

What special offers are currently available?

6 ONLINE SHOPPING
Descriptions and reviews

Getting started

1 What was the last electronic device you bought?
2 How did you choose which model to buy?
3 Where is the best place to get information about technological products?

A Classified ads

1 Complete the listings with these abbreviations.

a VGC (very good condition)   **c** RRP (recommended retail price)
b ONO (or nearest offer)   **d** BNIB (brand new in box)

| Find | audio and video | ⊗ | in | Didsbury | ⊗ | in | Manchester | ⊗ | Search | 🔍 |

Wharfedale sys5000 Hi-Fi
Wharfedale Hi-Fi for sale, £140 **1** ....! Includes CD player, USB port etc. Used but **2** .... CD lens could do with clean.
1 day ago   **£140**

Cambridge dacmagic 100 3 ....
Unused Cambridge dacmagic (**4** ....: £200). Unwanted gift. Grab a bargain! Reasonable offers considered.
1 day ago   **£150**

Apple iPad – immaculate condition boxed & sealed
Apple iPad for sale. Used once. As new with 6 months' warranty left. Comes with £30 case. Cash on collection only.
3 days ago   **£320**

JVC camcorder and bag
Comes with everything you need in original box, charger, leads. Will throw in batteries too. Open to offers.
3 days ago   **£125**

Sony RX100 camera with LCJRXA case
3 wks old, purchased brand new. Comes with original box, charger, USB cable. Some minor scratches on LCD screen, otherwise good working order.
3 days ago   **£375**

Apple iPhone
Black iPhone – selling due to upgrade. Unlocked to any network. Small crack on outer casing and other marks from everyday wear and tear, doesn't affect how it works.
3 day ago   **£80**

---

2 Study the listings again and find the following information.

1 Which item has never been used?

....

2 Which items have some cosmetic damage?

....

3 Which items can be bought at a lower price than advertised?

....

4 Which items come with accessories?

....

3 Can these people find what they want in the listings?

1 Jean wants a second hand iPhone in mint condition. ....

2 Paolo wants a camcorder with accessories. ....

3 Carlos wants an iPad in mint condition. ....

4 Stefan wants a stereo that is still under warranty. ....

4 Find words or phrases in the ads with the following meanings.

1 a long, thin break (noun) ....

2 marks made by something sharp (noun) ....

3 damage due to general use (3 word expression) ....

4 perfect (adjective) ....

5 needs (phrasal verb) ....

6 exchange old model for a new model (verb) ....

7 include for free (phrasal verb) ....

8 manufacturer's promise to repair or replace faulty item (noun) ....

5 Complete the listings below with words from the box.

upgraded	working order	bargain	BNIB
wear and tear	open	as new	

Jawbone Jambox
Bought just 3 months ago, so used, but **1** .... £80.00 (RRP: £120). **2** .... to offers.

Sony 3 CD Changer Stereo
Radio works fine but CD drawer won't open. Cost £250, now selling for £20.
A **3** .... if you know how to fix it!

4 .... Apple iPod Touch
Latest model in pink. Unused – unwanted gift. Full **5** .... – all accessories included. £260 ONO.

Two Sharp 40W speakers
Have had these for about 5 years and recently **6** .... Some cosmetic **7** ...., but still great sound. £30. Reasonable offers considered.

WHAT HI★FI?

Best Reviews to Help you Choose

Search

HOME	REVIEWS	NEWS	BLOGS	FORUMS	SHOP

Reviews > Technology > Stereo Systems > Denon > DSD-710AE

DSD-710AE

Write your own review

On the plus side …
- Clear detailed sound
- Even tonal balance
- Sturdy build and neat appearance

On the minus side …
- Sounds too polite and dynamically restrained

1 The only Denon disc-spinners we've come across in the past few months have been the Blu-ray-playing variety. So it's nice to get to grips with a new two-channel deck.

2 The styling is similar to that of the company's Blu-ray machines, but that's no bad thing. The partly sloping fascia, tidy button arrangement and black finish give the '710AE a very sophisticated air.

3 The player uses Denon's vibration and noise-resistant design that boasts extra rigidity and shorter signal paths. The USB input on the front allows you to play WMA and MP3 digital music files; it also works with (and charges) your iPod or iPhone.

4 And, the control system works very well. The remote control has dedicated keys that help you to scroll through the iPod menus and select tracks.

5 Granted, you need to be in close proximity to the iPod's screen to make the most of this functionality, but it's a nice touch and tunes played through the input sound enjoyable enough.

Detail, clarity and insight

6 'Enjoyable enough' is a phrase that you'll find yourself using after spending some time in the company of the '710AE. Which is strange, because if you're looking for gaping holes in the Denon's sonic ability, you're hard-pressed to find them.

7 It does a fine job at unravelling layers of detail; the clarity and insight on offer is a match for the likes of the Cambridge Audio Azur 650C, with no trace of coloration in the midrange, brightness in the treble or looseness in the bass.

8 The '710AE handles the heavy bassline of Notorious BIG's ***Mo Money Mo Problems*** with great aplomb. Vocals sound clear and detailed and the machine shows no sign of a struggle keeping up with the frisky tempo of Diana Ross's ***I'm Coming Out*** sample.

A tendency to hold back

9 Switch to more classical music, and it's easier to pinpoint an area where the class-leaders have an edge.

10 The first 30 seconds of the ***Theme From Jurassic Park*** are handled confidently enough, but, just as you expect the music to blossom, the Denon holds back.

11 This dynamic flaw means the player struggles to keep you entertained long-term and, although there's nothing offensive about its overall character, this niggle is enough to hold the Denon to a four-star rating.

B   Product reviews

1   Read the *What HI-FI?* description of the music system and choose the best summary.

1   The Denon DCD-710AE plays high and low music well, but struggles with faster music.

2   The Denon DCD-710AE sounds fantastic. It's a shame it looks so ugly.

3   The Denon DCD-710AE plays many kinds of music well, but in time gets boring to listen to.

4   The Denon DCD-710AE is good, but the Cambridge Audio Azur 650C is better value.

2   Read the sentences and put a tick in the correct column.

	True	False	No information
1 The machine plays both CDs and Blu-rays.	....	....	....
2 The reviewer likes the appearance of the machine.	....	....	....
3 This is the cheapest stereo currently available by Denon.	....	....	....
4 Digital music files sound as good as CDs when played on the machine.	....	....	....
5 To use the remote control on your iPod or iPhone, you have to stand close by.	....	....	....
6 The sound quality is not as good as the Cambridge Audio Azur 650C.	....	....	....
7 The machine didn't play Diana Ross's fast song *I'm Coming Out* well.	....	....	....
8 Classical music played on the machine didn't sound exciting.	....	....	....

3   Read paragraphs 2, 6, 7, 8, 10 and 11. Do they express a positive or negative opinion? Note down the words and phrases that helped you decide.

Reading tip

When recording vocabulary from a text, don't just write a list. Categorize the words. This way, you will have a useful bank of words with a similar theme. For example, you could categorize the vocabulary from the text on page 32 under the headings: 'Sound and Music' and 'Technology'. You could also categorize the functional phrases under the headings 'Giving positive opinions' and 'Giving negative opinions'.

Next steps

Choose a phone or camera, and find three online listings for it on a site such as eBay or Gumtree. How does the price and condition differ?

Read some online reviews about products you own. Do you agree with the reviews?

7 DETAILED INFORMATION
Operating instructions and warranties

Getting started

1   Do you enjoy cooking? What gadgets do you use in the kitchen?

2   Do you read instructions when you buy a new gadget, or do you try and work it out for yourself?

3   Have you ever returned a gadget because it was faulty?

A   Operating instructions

1   Read the introduction for *Swirl Supreme 6000* on page 35. What does it do?

a   It makes iced desserts

b   It makes and crushes ice

c   It allows you to carry frozen food around

2   Complete the gaps in the text with the following link words.

before	hence	if	even if
by	otherwise	once	as

Language note

It's important to use link words to understand the relationship between two parts of a sentence.

A second clause may represent a cause, a consequence, a condition, an additional piece of information or a description of how or why you do something.

*The recipe won't work **unless you follow the instructions**.* (condition)

*Melt the chocolate **by placing it in a bowl over a saucepan of hot water**.* (description)

3   Read the rest of the text about the Swirl Supreme 6000 and complete the sentences by writing up to five words in each space. Do not use the exact words from the text.

1   The function of the freezer bowl is to ....

2   The freezer bowl is ready to use if you shake it and ....

3   Because the volume of ingredients increases during freezing, always use less ....

4   If you wish to store completed desserts in the freezer, use ....

5   If using low fat milk instead of cream, you should expect the .... to be different.

Cookman's
Swirl Supreme 6000

Congratulations! You've just purchased a Swirl Supreme 6000. In no time at all, you'll be creating healthy and delicious chilled treats!

Parts:
- Easy-lock lid with spout
- Freezer bowl with double insulated wall and cooling liquid
- Base with non-slip rubber feet and heavy-duty motor
- Mixing paddle

Before you start

1 .... you begin, wrap the freezer bowl in a plastic bag and place in the back of the freezer where it is coldest. Freeze for between 6 and 22 hours, depending on the temperature of your freezer. To determine whether the cooling liquid is completely frozen, shake it. If you do not hear liquid moving, the cooling liquid is frozen and can be used.

How to Use the Swirl Supreme

Remove freezer bowl from freezer and place inside base.

Important: Use freezer bowl immediately as it will start to thaw straight away once removed.

Attach the mixing paddle into the drive unit and fit the easy-lock lid **2** .... rotating it clockwise until the triangular tabs on the lid and base are aligned.

Press the on/off switch. The bowl will turn.

Pour ingredients through spout.

3 .... using a recipe other than those in the enclosed booklet, ensure the yield does not exceed 1.5 quarts, as the mixture will increase in volume during the freezing process.

Wait 20–30 minutes, or until the mixture has thickened to your liking. Remove from bowl and serve. A

For a firmer consistency, transfer to an airtight container and store in the freezer for at least two hours. Do not freeze inside the freezer bowl **4** .... the mixture will stick to the sides and may damage it.

Tips

- Add chocolate chips and nuts **5** .... the mixture has begun to thicken, about 5 minutes before completion.

- Be aware that your desserts may have some different characteristics from store-bought desserts and drinks. B

- You can substitute the heavy creams and whole milks used in the recipes for healthier alternatives, but note that this may change the consistency and flavour. C Remember to always maintain the same quantities of your substituted ingredient as the original **6** .... it may impede the freezing process.

- Always test the ripeness of fruit before use. D Reduce the amount of sugar if fruit is ripe or sweet.

- If using artificial sweeteners instead of sugar, note that heat will affect the sweetness, **7** .... they should only be added to mixtures that have completely cooled. E

- Do not operate the unit for longer than 40 minutes, **8** .... the mixture is not yet solid. F

4 Choose the best location in the text (A–F) on page 35 for the following sentences. One sentence is not used.

1 Sweetness is reduced during freezing, so you may want to add more sugar if it is tart.

2 The higher the percentage of fat, the richer and softer the ice cream will be.

3 Ice cream mixtures must be liquid when first added to the unit. Do not use stiff mixtures such as whipped cream or frozen liquids.

4 Use wooden, plastic or rubber utensils, as metal utensils may damage the freezer bowl.

5 Possible reasons for failure to freeze include: the freezer bowl not being cold enough, the mixture being too warm or the proportion of ingredients being incorrect.

6 This is due to the fact that only fresh ingredients are used, rather than preservatives.

7 If a recipe requires you to heat a mixture in order for sugar to dissolve, omit this step and stir directly into the cold mixture.

5 Select vocabulary from the text, including the sentences in question 4 above, to complete the recipes below.

LOW-FAT PEACH FROZEN YOGURT

This dessert has such a creamy **1** ...., you'll never believe it is low in fat. Drain 1 can of peaches, reserve the juice and puree the peaches in a blender. Add 4 cups yogurt, peach juice and ¼ cup sugar. Blend until combined. Pour into freezer bowl and let it mix until it **2** ....

STRAWBERRY ICE CREAM

A delicious treat. Finely chop 1½ cups of strawberries. This will **3** .... around 1 cup of chopped strawberries. Heat 1 cup of heavy cream and 2 cups of milk in a saucepan.

Alternatively, use the same **4** .... of lower fat varieties. Beat 2 egg yolks with ½ cup of sugar, and gradually add to the mixture, stirring continuously. Once it has thickened, allow to cool. Add strawberries and mix for 25 minutes. You can **5** .... frozen strawberries for fresh ones out of season.

PINK GRAPEFRUIT SORBET

This **6** .... but sweet grapefruit sorbet is fresh and full of zing. Combine 2 cups of water with 2 cups of sugar in a pan and boil until the sugar **7** .... Then add 1½ cups of grapefruit juice. Cool completely then pour into freezer bowl and let it mix until it has turned to slush. Transfer to an **8** .... container and place in freezer until firm.

6 Which two of the following utensils are not required in any of the recipes above?

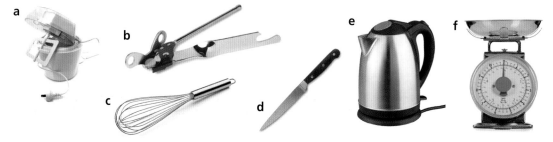

a b c d e f

B   Procedures

 Use the warranty information to answer the FAQs below. Answer *yes*, *no* or *not given*.

Cookman's
One (1) year limited warranty

Cookman Acquisition Corporation warrants to the original purchaser-owner of this new product that it is free from defects in materials and workmanship under normal home use for one year from the documented date of purchase. To register ownership of your *Swirl Supreme 6000*, please mail in the Warranty Registration Card. We suggest that you register promptly to facilitate verification of the date of original purchase. However, return of the product registration is not a condition of this warranty.

We will repair or replace any part of a defective product, provided that it has not been abused, misused, altered or damaged in any way after purchase. These warranties expressly exclude defects or damages caused by accessories or replacement parts other than those manufactured by Cookman's.

Should a defect develop within a year of normal use, you may return it for repair or replacement. Mail the part together with $14.00 for base, $6.00 for lid and freezer bowl, or $2.00 per paddle, whichever is applicable, for shipping, handling and insurance. Please enclose along with the above your name and return address. Mail to Cookmans Holdings, PO Box 5738, Reefers Hill, California, 84795. The handling fee is waived for California residents who need only supply proof of purchase. Please call 1-800-945-0078 for shipping instructions. We recommend that you use Certified Mail Delivery for the item(s) you are returning. That way you will receive a receipt stamped with the date of mailing and a unique article number that allows you to track and verify delivery online. Cookman's cannot be held responsible for in-transit damage or for packages that are not delivered to us. Lost and/or damaged products are not covered under warranty.

For customers in Canada, please send your handling per item fee in <u>US Funds only</u>. Canada Post money orders can be issued in US Funds for your convenience. We recommend you use an equivalent recorded delivery service for shipping.

---

1 Is it necessary to register in order to use my warranty? ....

2 My Swirl Supreme 6000 stopped working soon after I bought a replacement paddle from Cookman's. Is the warranty valid? ....

3 Will the replacement parts sent by Cookman's be insured against damage during transit? ....

4 Is the warranty valid for customers outside North America? ....

5 I'm from California. Do I need to send you anything? ....

6 Do I have to use Certified Mail? ....

7 I'm Canadian. Can I pay in Canadian dollars? ....

Next steps

Next time you buy something which has instructions in several languages, try reading them in English first. Translate them into your own language, and compare your answer to the text in the instructions.

8 HEALTH AND SAFETY
Warning labels, leaflets and letters

Getting started

1 What household items need warning labels?

2 Do you understand these warnings?

3 Have you also seen warnings sent in the post or via email?

A Warnings

1 What household items are the warnings 1–3 for? Choose three from the box.

peanuts	skin cream	bleach
pills	washing-up liquid	paint

1 .... 2 .... 3 ....

1

FLAMMABLE

Contains cobalt bis (2-ethylhexanoate) and ethyl methyl ketoxime. May produce an allergic reaction. Keep away from sources of ignition - no smoking.
Repeat exposure may cause skin dryness or cracking. Ensure maximum ventilation during application and drying. Avoid contact with the skin and eyes.
In case of contact with eyes, rinse immediately with plenty of water and seek medical advice.
After contact with skin, wash immediately with plenty of soap and water, or a quality skin cleaner.

DO NOT USE SOLVENT OR THINNERS

Restrict interior use to small surface areas such as doors, window frames and skirting boards. Not recommended for interior use on large surface areas – walls, floors in confined spaces. If swallowed seek medical advice immediately and show this container or label. Keep out of the reach of children.
Safety data sheet available for professional user on request.

2

Do not take:

- If you have severe liver disease
- If you are pregnant
- With any other paracetamol-containing products

Talk to your pharmacist or doctor if you are breastfeeding.

Immediate medical advice should be sought in the event of an overdose.

If you need to take this medicine continuously for more than 3 days **it can make headaches worse.** If symptoms persist, consult your doctor.
Do not give to children under 6.
Do not exceed the stated dose.

Keep all medicines out of the sight and reach of children.

3

WARNING

KEEP AWAY FROM CHILDREN. KEEP AWAY FROM EYES. IF PRODUCT GETS INTO EYES, RINSE THOROUGHLY WITH WATER. PEOPLE WITH SENSITIVE OR DAMAGED SKIN SHOULD AVOID PROLONGED CONTACT WITH THE PRODUCT. IF PRODUCT IS INGESTED THEN SEEK MEDICAL ADVICE. NOT SUITABLE FOR USE ON CLOTHING OR FABRICS.

2 Complete the chart by ticking the products where the statements are true.

	Product 1	Product 2	Product 3
Store away from children.			
Wash if it gets on the skin.			
Go to the doctor if swallowed.			

3 Read the sentences and put a tick in the correct column.

		True	False	No information
1	Product 1 catches fire easily.	…………	…………	…………
2	Product 1 is only suitable for indoor use.	…………	…………	…………
3	Pregnant women should only use product 2 for a maximum of 3 days.	…………	…………	…………
4	Product 2 may only be used for more than 3 days under a doctor's supervision.	…………	…………	…………
5	Some people's skin may be affected by product 3.	…………	…………	…………
6	Don't wash clothes with product 3.	…………	…………	…………

4 Complete the warnings with words from the warnings in exercise 1. The first letter is given.

Caution

Do not
1 i…………

Warning

2 f…………
liquid

Seek medical help immediately if the stated
3 d………… is exceeded.

Avoid
4 p…………
exposure to sunlight

Ensure adequate
5 v…………
when using this product

If product comes into contact with eyes,
6 r…………
immediately

Factsheet: The health risks of second-hand smoke

How does second-hand smoke affect health?

Previously, people often only considered second-hand smoke as a welfare issue, focusing on the smell and the irritation that tobacco smoke causes to eyes, nose and throat. But now the weight of evidence for much more serious risks to health from second-hand smoke has grown too great to ignore.

Why is one person's smoking harmful to others?

Tobacco smoke contains around 4,000 chemicals, including arsenic, benzene, formaldehyde and ammonia. Around 60 of these chemicals are known or suspected to cause cancer. Many of the toxic chemicals are actually more concentrated in the smoke that's given off by the burning tip of a cigarette (sidestream smoke) than in the smoke inhaled by the smoker through the filter (mainstream smoke). Around 85 per cent of the smoke in a room where people are smoking is the more toxic sidestream smoke. By breathing in the smoke in the atmosphere, the non-smoker is exposed to many of the same health risks as the smoker.

What are the health risks?

- **Lung cancer**

The best known risk to smokers, lung cancer, is also more common in people regularly exposed to second-hand smoke. The Government's Scientific Committee on Tobacco and Health (SCOTH) reported in 1998 that exposure to second-hand smoke increases the risk of lung cancer in non-smokers by 20–30 per cent.[1]

- **Heart disease**

Even though they inhale only 1% of the smoke, non-smokers exposed to second-hand smoke may suffer 25 per cent of the increased risk of heart disease associated with active smoking (one recent study suggests it might be as much as 50 per cent).[2] Just 30 minutes of breathing second-hand smoke can reduce the coronary blood supply of a non-smoker to the same level as that of a smoker.[3]

- **Stroke**

A study in New Zealand found that exposure to second-hand smoke increases the risk of stroke by 82 per cent in non-smokers.[4] This is a serious concern, as stroke is such a common condition.

- **Asthma**

Around 3.4 million people in the UK have asthma and for most of these, tobacco smoke is a trigger for an asthma attack. For someone with asthma, just one hour of exposure to second-hand smoke can cause a 20 per cent deterioration in lung function.[5]

- **Pregnancy complications**

Breathing in second-hand smoke during pregnancy increases the risk of having a baby with a low birth weight. Small babies are at much greater risk of infections and other health problems.[6]

- **Risks to children**

Children don't make up much of the workforce, of course, but they may still spend quite a bit of time in other people's workplaces, like schools, leisure centres, cafes or shopping centres. Children are even more at risk because of their smaller lungs and the fact that their bodies are still developing. For them, exposure to second-hand smoke increases the risk of asthma, bronchitis, pneumonia and middle ear disease.

Conclusion

After reviewing all the available evidence, the latest report prepared for the Government by SCOTH has concluded that there is now no doubt that breathing in other people's smoke significantly increases the risk of cancer and heart disease, and advises that no infant, child or adult should be exposed to second-hand smoke.[7]

A recent review of international research on the immediate health impact of smokefree workplace legislation found rapid and dramatic improvements. Air quality, respiratory health and levels of heart attacks and heart disease all improved substantially within months of the legislation being introduced.[8]

Reproduced with permission from the Public Health Agency
For references, see acknowledgments on page 127.

1 Scan the leaflet issued by the Public Health Agency opposite.

1 Identify four chemicals found in cigarette smoke.

2 Identify four illnesses caused by smoking.

2 Read the leaflet again, and complete the sentences. Choose the answer which is explicitly given in the text.

1 There has been greater focus on the dangers of second-hand smoke since …

   a the government accepted it as a welfare issue.

   b overwhelming proof of its dangers emerged.

   c people realized the irritation it caused to eyes, nose and throat.

2 Sidestream smoke …

   a has a higher proportion of dangerous chemicals than inhaled smoke.

   b contains 4,000 chemicals, 60 of which are known to cause cancer.

   c contains 85% of the chemicals found in inhaled smoke.

3 Lung cancer …

   a affects 20–30% of non-smokers.

   b is the most common disease in non-smokers that is caused by second-hand smoke.

   c is 20–30% more likely to occur if people are exposed to second-hand smoke.

4 People exposed to second-hand smoke for 30 minutes …

   a are 25–50% more likely to get heart disease than people who are unexposed.

   b experience the same reduced blood supply to the heart as that of a smoker.

   c experience a 25–50% reduction in coronary blood supply.

5 In New Zealand, it was discovered that …

   a people exposed to second-hand smoke are 82% more likely to get a stroke.

   b 82% of people exposed to second-hand smoke suffer from a stroke.

   c the risk of stroke to second-hand smoke is 82% of the risk of stroke to smokers.

6 The article states that …

   a most asthma attacks are triggered by second-hand smoke.

   b 20% of asthma sufferers are exposed to second-hand smoke.

   c lung function of asthma sufferers decreases by 20% when exposed to second-hand smoke.

7 Children are at greater risk of second-hand smoke …

   a because they spend a lot of time in public places.

   b due to the size of their lungs and their stage of development.

   c if they already suffer from asthma, bronchitis, pneumonia or middle ear disease.

Reading tip

Take time to read the sentences carefully and really understand what the numbers mean.

C Written warnings

1 Read the three letters received by Mark Cox. Identify the senders.

landlord	gas company	employer	bank

1 ....   2 ....   3 ....

1

DISCONNECTION WARNING

This letter serves as a final notice, as you have not responded to our two previous requests to obtain a meter reading at the above address.

To ensure accurate billing, utility services are obligated to take a meter reading a minimum of once every six months. Should access to the equipment be denied, the service provider has the right to disconnect the service. Please arrange for our employees to access the meter at your property within 10 working days from the date shown above, otherwise we will have no option but to act accordingly. Reconnection incurs a $200 charge which will be added to your account after your service is restored.

Please call 1-800-674-3948 at your earliest convenience to arrange a visit from one of our service engineers.

2

Dear Mr Cox,

This letter is to remind you that smoking is not permitted in your apartment unit. An outdoor smoking area has been designated at the rear of the apartment building. You entered into this agreement when you signed the lease. We have received a complaint of second-hand smoke infiltrating the hallway outside your unit on 5th August. We are requesting that you take immediate steps to ensure that you, your family and any guests or visitors you have do not smoke in your apartment unit in accordance with your tenancy agreement.

Should there be any further incident or circumstances with respect to smoking in your unit, we will serve you with a notice to terminate your tenancy early.

3

Dear Mr Cox,

Subject: written warning: unprofessional conduct – insubordination

On 4th August you refused to attend a staff meeting and indicated you 'did not feel like it.' This behaviour is considered insubordination under University of Peterfield policy B025 Disciplinary / Professional. This type of unprofessional conduct cannot be tolerated in the workplace.

Please be advised that unless immediate and sustained improvement in your behaviour is realized, you will be subject to further disciplinary action up to and including termination of employment.

2 Identify the following three pieces of information in each letter.

    a What Mark is being warned about.

    b The action Mark must take.

    c The consequence if Mark takes no action.

3 Match the verb to its meaning (in this context).

1	respond *(letter 1)*	**a**	not allow
2	deny *(letter 1)*	**b**	reply
3	restore *(letter 1)*	**c**	end
4	terminate *(letter 2)*	**d**	achieve
5	tolerate *(letter 3)*	**e**	return to normal
6	realize *(letter 3)*	**f**	allow

Language note

Remember that 'if' is not the only word to show the relationship between condition and consequence. 'Unless', 'otherwise', 'should', 'failure to' and 'provided that' can also have this function. Notice how some of these are used in Mark's three letters.

4 Complete the rules and warnings below with 'should', 'unless', 'failure to' or 'provided that'. Look at how these words are used in the example sentences to help you.

1 .... means 'except if'.

Example: .... *you pay the balance immediately, we will shut down your account.*

2 .... refers to the action of not doing something you should do.

Example: .... *follow these guidelines may result in injury.*

3 .... means 'only if' and is used in conjunction with a permissive consequence.

Example: *You can use the tools* .... *you take good care of them.*

4 .... means 'if' but is followed by a verb in the infinitive form.

Example: *I don't mind paying a deposit* .... *it be necessary.*

Language note

Note how different modal verbs are used in the public health leaflet (page 40) and the warning letter (page 42). The public health warning used *can*, *may* and *might*. This is because scientific statistics are never fully definite. The warning letters use *must* and *will* because in these circumstances the consequences of an action are definite.

Next steps

Do an online search for 'public health warnings'. What sorts of health hazards are people being warned about at the moment?

9 HOLIDAY PLANS
Trip itineraries and details

Getting started

1 Where was the last place you visited on holiday?
2 Where do you get information about places you want to visit?
3 What information do you need about a destination before you travel there?

A Travel itineraries

1 You are interested in going on holiday, and see this tour on a website. Give yourself one minute to scan the itinerary on the opposite page and complete the information below. Write 'not given' if the information is not in the text.

Length of tour: ....

Countries visited: ....

Cost: ....

Maximum number of tourists: ....

Reading tip

You can identify items which are *not* included in the price by the modal verb 'can', e.g. '[...] you can enjoy a mouthwatering steak ...'. Other phrases indicating the same thing include 'optional' or 'you've the chance / opportunity to ...'

---

2 Read the itinerary in more detail. Tick the excursions which are included in the tour price.

☐ guided tour of Buenos Aires
☐ tango show
☐ football match

☐ excursion to Iguazú Falls
☐ boat trip below Iguazú Falls
☐ cable car trip up Sugar Loaf Mountain

3 Your friend emails you some questions about the holiday. Which questions are answered in the text? Make a note of the answers, where possible.

1 What time will my flight from the UK arrive in Buenos Aires?
2 Do all the hotels have pools?
3 How many flights will I take during the course of the trip?
4 Will I see the Iguazú Falls from the Argentinean side or the Brazilian side?
5 Is it possible to go up the Corcovado Mountain and go to the samba show?
6 Which meals are included in the trip price?

DISCOVERY JOURNEYS
Small Group Journeys

ARGENTINA & BRAZIL
GOLONDRINA JOURNEY:
SHORT BREAK TO BUENOS AIRES, RIO AND THE IGUAZÚ FALLS

| OVERVIEW | ITINERARY | DATES & PRICES | TRIP DOSSIER | REVIEWS |

GOLONDRINA JOURNEY

Summary of nights: Buenos Aires 2; Iguazú 2; Rio de Janeiro 2.

- A short, adventurous journey to 3 of South America's most iconic highlights.
- Sophistication, grace and vitality – Buenos Aires has them all in spades.
- Iguazú Falls, the continent's most powerful natural phenomenon.
- Rio de Janeiro, city of fun, music, dance, football, beaches and uplifting views.

UK clients depart on direct overnight flight arriving in Buenos Aires, Argentina, early morning on day 1.

Day 1 Sat. Guided tour of this buzzy city's highlights including the colonial centre; time to explore on your own. Optional night out at a tango show – an exotic treat!

Day 2 Your chance to see more of the city – its museums, parks, pavement cafés, the classy redevelopment of the old port where you can enjoy a mouthwatering steak for a fraction of the UK cost. Later, you've the chance to attend one of the city's exuberant Sunday football matches, if there's a good one on.

Day 3 Fly (2hrs) to **Puerto Iguazú** in the subtropical northeast. Explore the pleasant little town or relax by the pool in your hotel's leafy garden.

Day 4 Excursion to the Argentinian side of the **Iguazú Falls** where you can follow walkways above, alongside and behind the immense veils of water. You can even take a boat trip close to the falls to be drenched by the spray!

Day 5 Visit the Brazilian side and British-run bird park before flying to **Rio de Janeiro** (approx 2 hrs).

Day 6 Excursion up the **Sugar Loaf** by cable car to enjoy the panoramic views, and if you can't get enough of the views take an optional trip up the Corcovado Mountain by train. Otherwise there is time to hang out on the beach or in a bar, visit the tropical Botanical Gardens or watch a samba show over a few ice-cold caipirinhas.

Day 7 Depart for international flight or extension.

UK clients leave on a direct flight home the following day, Sat.

Trip Profile
Transport: 2 flights (2hrs each).
Accommodation: Friendly mid-range hotels, with private bathroom.
Meals: Breakfast daily.
Included excursions: Buenos Aires city tour; Argentinian and Brazilian sides of the Iguazú falls; Sugar Loaf Mountain, Rio.
Group size: Min 4, max 16. Led by Journey Latin America tour leader.

A few days to spare?
Extend your trip by adding on a few days at the beginning or end of your tour on a tailor-made, private basis. Have a look at our most popular extensions to the Golondrina Journey or contact one of our consultants for more inspiring ideas.

Length of tour: ....
Countries visited: ....
....
Cost: ....
Max. No. of tourists: ....

Single Travellers

There is no extra cost for single travellers who are willing to share a room. You will be accommodated with another same-sex member of the group who is also travelling solo. For single travellers who wish to have their own room there are a limited number of single supplement places available, which carry a surcharge.

Accommodation

We should emphasize that on our Discovery Journeys the standard of accommodation varies. We aim to keep the price competitive while ensuring the basic comforts. All hotels are clean and almost all will have a private bathroom with hot water. Examples of the hotels we use on the *Golondrina* include Hotel Waldorf in Buenos Aires, Hotel Orquideas in Puerto Iguazú and Hotel Copacabana Mar in Rio. These hotels are subject to change and are dependent on availability. Address and contact details will be sent out with your final documents.

Climate

In tropical Rio and Puerto Iguazú, December to March are the hottest and most humid months, with temperatures reaching 40°C, and rain which falls in brief, heavy showers. From June to September, temperatures are more moderate (18–23°C) and there is plenty of sunshine, but cold fronts can usher in periods of up to several days of cloud and drizzle. In Buenos Aires October, November, March and April see temperatures between 15 and 25°C and a good deal of sunshine, although rain is not uncommon. January and February are hot, around 30°C.

Money

The unit of currency in Brazil is the *real*, and in Argentina the *peso argentino*. A budget of around US$40 per day should cover the cost of meals, drinks and the odd souvenir. Cash machines are available in all major cities and towns, and in most shops and restaurants you can also pay by card. However, since cards can get lost, damaged, withheld or blocked, you should not rely exclusively on a card to access funds. We recommend that additionally you take a reasonable quantity of US dollars in cash, which you can exchange into local currency, and possibly some travellers' cheques (American Express are the most widely accepted).

Tipping

Tipping is expected and local guides often rely on their tip as a significant proportion of their income. Most service industry workers will expect a tip of some kind and so it is useful to have spare change for hotel porters, taxi drivers and the like. It is common to leave 10–12 per cent in restaurants. If you would like to show your appreciation for your Journey Latin America tour leader, that of course would be gratefully received.

Clothing and special equipment

For day-to-day wear you should take loose-fitting, breathable clothes. Comfortable shoes are important and sandals are useful. A sun hat, sunblock and sunglasses are necessary, and you should take a light fleece for cool nights and a Gore-Tex layer, as well as swimwear, a towel, insect repellent and a torch. At the Iguazú Falls you can get very wet from the spray. You may like to take dry clothes in a bag and simply wear swimwear and flip flops as it is hard to dry your clothes in the hotel. If you plan to go to good restaurants or out on evening entertainment trips, you might want to bring something a bit smarter as well.

B   A trip dossier

1   Your friend has made the following notes about the holiday but not all of them are accurate. Correct any false statements.

Brazil/Argentina trip – things to remember

1. Request a single room – there's no extra charge!   . . . .

2. Note – hotels might not have hot water!!   . . . .

3. We'll be staying at Hotel Waldorf, Hotel Orquídeas & Hotel Copacabana Mar – pass on addresses to Mum & Dad   . . . .

4. Weather likely to be wet in March – take waterproofs!   . . . .

5. Meals are included in tour price – no need to budget that in.   . . . .

6. Take debit card, US dollars and maybe some traveller's cheques (American Express)   . . . .

7. Need money for tips – 10%. Also may want to tip the tour leader.   . . . .

8. Take swimming costume and flip flops for Iguazú Falls trip.   . . . .

Language note

Some texts need to give instructions in a polite and welcoming way. 'Must' and the imperative form tend not to be used as they sound authoritative and unfriendly. Other phrases like 'You should ...' and 'It is recommended ...' are used instead. Readers, however, should treat these as instructions, not suggestions.

---

2   The 'Useful information' sheet provides lots of instructions that are not in the imperative form. Note any you can find and check them in the answer key.

3   The highlighted words in the text have at least two different meanings. Use a dictionary and note the meaning of the words as they are used here.

1 solo (adj)   ....

2 carry (v)   ....

3 cover (v)   ....

4 odd (adj)   ....

5 blocked (adj)   ....

Next steps

Look at other itineraries on the Journey Latin America website **www.journeylatinamerica.co.uk**
Which tour would you most like to go on?

Find more vocabulary on the topics of clothes, weather and money using the dossier for your preferred trip.

10 UPDATES
Traffic and weather information

Getting started

1 Do you check traffic and weather information before you travel?
2 Where do you get this information?
3 Do you change your plans if the weather or traffic is bad?

A   Traffic information

1 **Look at the webpage. Circle the places you would click to get the following information.**

1 Details of a recent road closure on the A66.
2 How to get up-to-date traffic information sent directly to you by email.
3 Up-to-date traffic information on the M4 motorway.
4 Information about roadworks taking place in a month's time.

2 Match the vocabulary to its meaning.

1	incident	a	a traffic jam
2	congestion	b	a short road where vehicles join or leave a motorway
3	junction	c	an accident or unpleasant event
4	bound	d	where two or more roads meet
5	slip	e	going in the direction of

3 You are going on a walking holiday in the Peak District, a national park in central England. You want to take the M6 northbound from Junction 7 to Junction 15. You planned to travel at 10 p.m. on 9th July. Circle two problems that will affect you.

Road	Location	Direction	Description	Delay	Start Date/Time	End Date/Time
M6	J3 ↓ J3A	Northbound	⚠️ **Incident** **Obstructions - Broken down Vehicle** On the M6 northbound between junctions J3 and J3A, there are currently delays of 10 mins due to a broken down vehicle closing one lane. Normal traffic conditions expected from 3.45 p.m.	10 mins	N/A	10/07/2013 15:45
M6	J5	Northbound	⊖ **Future Road/Slip Closure** **Roadworks** The M6 northbound exit slip at junction J5 will be closed due to roadworks, from 9.30 p.m. on 10 July 2013 to 5.30 a.m. on 11 July 2013.	N/A	10/07/2013 21:30	11/07/2013 05:30
M6	J7	Northbound	⊖ **Future Road/Slip Closure** **Roadworks** The M6 northbound entry slip at junction J7 will be closed due to roadworks, between 9.30 p.m. and 5:30 am, from 8 July 2013 to 11 July 2013.	N/A	8/07/2013 21:30	11/07/2013 05:30
M6	J7 ↓ J8	Northbound	⊖ **Future Road/Slip Closure** **Roadworks** The M6 northbound will be closed between junctions J7 and J8 due to roadworks, between 9:30 pm and 5.30 a.m., from 8 July 2013 to 11 July 2013.	N/A	8/07/2013 21:30	11/07/2013 05:30
M6	J8	Southbound	⊖ **Future Road/Slip Closure** **Roadworks** The M6 northbound will be closed at junction J8 due to roadworks, between 9.30 p.m. and 5.30 a.m., from 9 July 2013 to 11 July 2013.	N/A	9/07/2013 21:30	11/07/2013 05:30
M6	J16	Northbound	⊖ **Current Road/Slip Closure** **Accident - Vehicle Recovery** The M6 northbound entry slip at junction J16 is closed, due to vehicle recovery. Road expected to re-open from 7.30 p.m.	N/A	N/A	10/07/2013 19:30

4 Read the traffic information in more detail and answer the questions below.

1 It usually takes Dan 20 minutes to travel to work between junctions 3 and 3A. How long will it take if he travels immediately today?

2 It usually takes Julie 40 minutes to travel to work between junctions 3 and 3A. She starts work at 1.00 p.m. What time should she leave home today to get to work on time?

3 John lives near junction 5. He's going to a party on 10th July at his friend's house, near junction 4. He wants to leave at 7 p.m., and get home just before midnight. Can he use the motorway to drive to and from the party?

4 Wayne plans to drive between junction 7 and junction 10 on 9th July. What is the earliest time he can use the motorway?

5 Can Lucy drive from junction 8 to junction 5 at 3 a.m. on 11th July?

B Weather information

 Skim read the two weather reports for the Brecon Beacons National Park in Wales. What will be the biggest weather problem on each day – snow, rain, wind or fog?

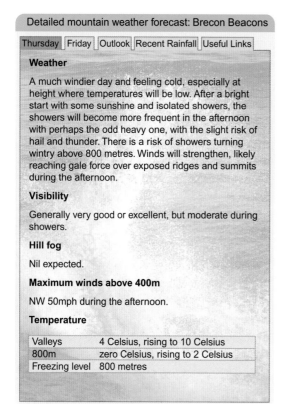

Detailed mountain weather forecast: Brecon Beacons

Thursday | Friday | Outlook | Recent Rainfall | Useful Links

Weather

A much windier day and feeling cold, especially at height where temperatures will be low. After a bright start with some sunshine and isolated showers, the showers will become more frequent in the afternoon with perhaps the odd heavy one, with the slight risk of hail and thunder. There is a risk of showers turning wintry above 800 metres. Winds will strengthen, likely reaching gale force over exposed ridges and summits during the afternoon.

Visibility

Generally very good or excellent, but moderate during showers.

Hill fog

Nil expected.

Maximum winds above 400m

NW 50mph during the afternoon.

Temperature

Valleys	4 Celsius, rising to 10 Celsius
800m	zero Celsius, rising to 2 Celsius
Freezing level	800 metres

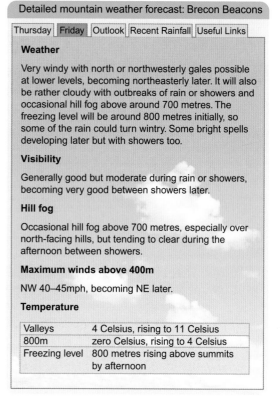

Detailed mountain weather forecast: Brecon Beacons

Thursday | Friday | Outlook | Recent Rainfall | Useful Links

Weather

Very windy with north or northwesterly gales possible at lower levels, becoming northeasterly later. It will also be rather cloudy with outbreaks of rain or showers and occasional hill fog above around 700 metres. The freezing level will be around 800 metres initially, so some of the rain could turn wintry. Some bright spells developing later but with showers too.

Visibility

Generally good but moderate during rain or showers, becoming very good between showers later.

Hill fog

Occasional hill fog above 700 metres, especially over north-facing hills, but tending to clear during the afternoon between showers.

Maximum winds above 400m

NW 40–45mph, becoming NE later.

Temperature

Valleys	4 Celsius, rising to 11 Celsius
800m	zero Celsius, rising to 4 Celsius
Freezing level	800 metres rising above summits by afternoon

Reading tip

Skim a text to get the general gist of it. Allow your eyes to pass over the text, always looking forward. Don't read every word.

Scan to get specific information. Again, don't read every word but pass your eyes over the text, looking out for specific keywords or information.

---

2 From the following list, choose two summaries that best describe the weather for Thursday and Friday.

1 Cold and windy with scattered showers increasing in the afternoon.
2 Cold winds with a strong likelihood of hail and thunder.
3 Cool and windy with sunny spells; should remain dry.
4 A cold, windy start to the day; winds dying down in the afternoon.
5 Strong winds and showers, with some brighter spells later on.

Thursday: ....   **Friday:** ....

3 Scan the texts. Write *Thursday, Friday* or *both days* in the spaces.

1 Views from the top of mountains will be better on ....

2 The wind direction will change on ....

3 The wind will get increasingly strong on ....

4 It may get foggy on top of the hills on ....

5 Short bursts of rain are expected on ....

4 Using the texts on page 50, decide which of the following weather conditions words 1–6 are usually associated with.

wind	rain	sun	temperature

1 low   ....

2 bright   ....

3 showers   ....

4 strengthen   ....

5 gale force   ....

6 outbreaks   ....

Language note

If something is possible, it may happen, or it may not. If something is probable, there is a good chance that it will happen.

5 Are the following weather conditions possible or probable? Note down the words and phrases that helped you decide.

1 A heavy shower on Thursday afternoon. ....

2 Hail and thunder on Thursday afternoon. ....

3 Gale force winds in some places on Thursday afternoon. ....

4 Cloudy and showery on Friday. ....

5 Wintry rain on Friday. ....

6 Less hill fog on Friday afternoon. ....

6 You receive this message from a friend who you plan to go hiking with. Which day is she talking about?

I'd bring your walking poles. They'll help keep you steady if things get too blustery. I don't think you'll need an extra fleece, though. I'm not going to bother taking binoculars, because I don't think there'll be much opportunity to use them. And don't forget waterproofs – you'll definitely need them!

Next steps

Go to the Traffic England website. Which motorway has the most traffic disruptions at the moment? **www.trafficengland.co.uk**

Go to the Met Office website, and find the best day to go walking in the Brecon Beacons this week. **www.metoffice.gov.uk/loutdoor/mountainsafety**

11 GUIDES
Sightseeing information

Getting started

1 Do you use a guidebook when you visit new places?
2 Where do you get information about places to visit?
3 What do you know about Sydney, Australia?

A Map reading

1 Look at the map of Sydney. What do you think the following abbreviations stand for?

1 ST (as in ARGYLE ST)   ....
2 LN (as in Kendall LN)   ....
3 HWY (as in BRADFIELD HWY)   ....
4 EXPWY (as in CAHILL EXPWY)   ....

2 Look at the map and note down words that describe coastal features. Can you guess their meaning by looking at the map?

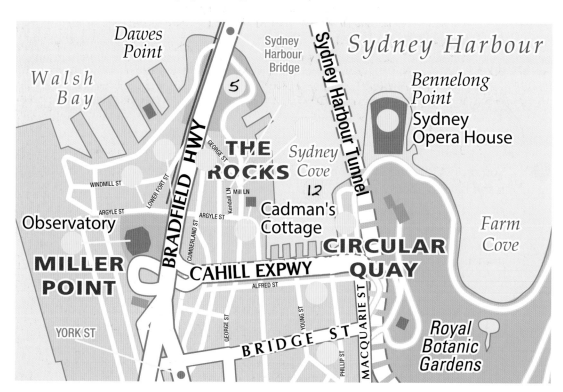

B   A guided walk

1   Read the guided walking tour of Sydney. Add numbers to the map to mark the places the walking tour visits. Two have been done for you.

Sydney Walking Tour: The Rocks and Circular Quay

For a window into Sydney's early days and a close encounter with the Sydney Opera House and Sydney Harbour Bridge, take a stroll through The Rocks and around Circular Quay.

1   Start your tour at Observatory Park 1 , where you can visit the old Sydney Observatory and take in some sweeping harbour views. At the base of the hill is The Garrison Church (corner of Argyle and Lower Fort Streets) 2 . Built in 1843, this is Australia's oldest church and where Australia's first prime minister Edmund Barton went to school. From here, wander down Argyle Street through the Argyle Cut (corner of Argyle Street and Bradfield Highway), a dramatic tunnel dug through the hillside by convicts 3 .

2   On the far side, head left onto Cumberland Street where you'll find BridgeClimb (5 Cumberland Street) 4 . If you're feeling brave, take a tour over the grand arch of the Sydney Harbour Bridge. Alternatively, climb the stairs from Cumberland Street onto the bridge's eastern footpath and visit the Pylon Lookout in the southeastern pylon 5 . Displays here document the bridge's construction during the 1920s and '30s.

3   Back on Argyle Street, head downhill and hang left onto Kendall Lane for the Rocks Discovery Museum (2–8 Kendall Lane) 6 . The intriguing exhibits here focus on early European artefacts and The Rocks' original residents, the Cadigal people.

4   From Kendall Lane, turn right onto Mill Lane and walk towards George Street 7 . If it's a Saturday or Sunday, The Rocks Market, the city's "premier" farmers and authentic Australian products marketplace, will be in full swing. Also here is Cadman's Cottage (110 George Street) 8 . Built in 1816, it is one of Sydney's oldest houses. John Cadman was a shipping officer at the fledgling harbour; his house later served as a sea captain's retirement home and police headquarters. Today it houses the Sydney Harbour National Park Information Centre.

5   Below Cadman's Cottage is Sydney Cove. Navigate your way around the shoreline to Circular Quay 9 , the hub of Sydney's public transportation system. From here, ferries, buses and trains will take you anywhere in the "Harbour City."

6   Just inland from Circular Quay is the sandstone Customs House (31 Alfred Street) 10 . Originally an import/export clearance hall, it's now a library and civic centre. Grab a coffee at Café Sydney on the roof, and inspect the 1:500 Sydney scale model built into the lobby floor.

7   Detour up Bridge Street to the Museum of Sydney (southwestern corner of Bridge and Phillip Streets) 11 , an outstanding multimedia museum documenting Sydney's places, people and development.

8   Back by the harbour, wander around Circular Quay East past a lively string of bars and eateries. Savour some local oysters, or just enjoy the photo-worthy views of the Sydney Harbour Bridge across Sydney Cove 12 .

9   Finish your tour on the steps of the iconic Sydney Opera House (Bennelong Point, Circular Quay East), Sydney's architectural masterpiece and No. 1 attraction 13 .

2 Which landmark from the guided walk is being described in these excerpts from a guide book?

1 Built on the ruins of the home of the first governor, Arthur Phillip, this museum uses state-of-the-art installations to explore the people, cultures and evolution of the city from its conception, through the colonial era to the modern day. Don't miss the giant showcase of items from the convict era. Panoramic views of the city from 1788 to the present are also displayed on video screens.

2 People have made illegal crossings since the 1950s, but now it's possible to scale this iconic monument at almost any time of day, except during electrical storms and strong winds. You're given a safety suit and a head-set, as well as an extensive training session before tackling the climb, during which you're secured with a harness. Tours last 3½ hours.

3 Tucked away on a side-street, this pocket-sized, family-friendly museum examines the history of the area from pre-European days to the present.
Four chronological displays cover Warrane (pre–1788), Colony (1788–1820), Port (1820–1900) and Transformations (1900 to the present), with careful attention paid to the region's original inhabitants. The museum is packed with artefacts, and the rolling videos will give tired feet a welcome rest.

4 Built on Sydney cove, and once the shipping centre of the city, this major transport hub is a focal point for commuters and tourists alike. You'll also find pleasant harbour walkways, parks, buskers and a wealth of diverse eateries. The Museum of Contemporary Art is located here, and the Sydney Opera House is just a short stroll away.

5 This stretch of road, which cuts dramatically through the ridge above, was first excavated by prisoners using hand tools. Work began in 1843 and was completed 24 years later with the aid of explosives. Now adorned with attractive greenery, a walk between the sheer hewn sandstone is especially atmospheric.

3 Use the information from both the walking tour and the guide book extracts to choose the best answer to these questions on a travel blog.

---

3 days ago

1 Is the Rock's Market open at weekends?

REPLY

a Yes, it is. But it's closed on weekdays. ☐

b No. It's only open on weekdays. ☐

Mark

---

1 week ago

2 Is it possible to board a boat at Circular Quay?

a No it's not for public use. ☐

b Yes, public ferries operate there. ☐

Margery

---

2 weeks ago

3 Where's a good place to get some seafood?

a I recommend Café Sydney on the top of Customs House. ☐

b I've heard there are some good places on the east end of Circular Quay. ☐

Jess

---

15 days ago

4 What's the difference between The Rocks Discovery Museum and the Sydney Museum?

a The Rocks Museum covers natural history and local geography, while the Sydney museum covers colonial history. ☐

b The Rocks Museum is dedicated to both European and local history, while the Sydney Museum is only about local history. ☐

Susie

---

4 Choose an alternative word from the text on page 53 to replace the word in italics.

1 Pause a while on the bridge to *appreciate* the sights, sounds and smells.
(paragraph 1) ....

2 Early evening is the perfect time to *take a stroll* along the quay.
(paragraph 1) ....

3 When you get to the end of the street, *turn* left.
(paragraph 3) ....

4 Why not *take a roundabout route* through the park on the way to the museum?
(paragraph 7) ....

Next steps

Find some guided walks of cities you know on the National Geographic website:

http://travel.nationalgeographic.co.uk/travel/city-guides

Next time you visit a city that features on this website, try one of the guided walks.

12 TALES OF ADVENTURE
Blogs and forums

Getting started

1 What activities do you like to do when on holiday?

2 How do your friends let you know what activities they've been doing?

3 Do you follow any blogs written by people you've never met?

A A travel website

1 Skim the posts on *Travel Tales* and note what each person has been doing. Then decide which comment is most appropriate and write a, b or c.

Annie: ..... Ela: ..... Charlene: .....

Travel Tales

Home | Friends | Profile

Annie Wu

Great start to the year ... spent this morning snorkelling around a shipwreck and swam with turtles! Bought a fantastic new sarong, then got ready for the show. Spent two hours performing, then time for an evening dip!

a Sounds like you're having a great holiday!
b I want your job ☺
c You're so brave! You'd never catch me doing that in a million years!

Ela Oldham

Officially had the maddest day of my life ever, bar none! Went on a tour abseiling and zip-wiring through the world's tallest rainforest in Costa Rica. Longest zip wire was half a mile long. Everyone else on the tour was a pensioner; I was the youngest by over 40 years. Half way down, the heavens opened and we ended up drenched, whizzing over the rainforest in the thunder and lightning!

a Can't believe you're doing that at your age ☺
b Wow, can't imagine my nan doing that!
c Sorry to hear it didn't go according to plan.

Charlene Thompson

Plucked up the courage to go scuba diving at last. Can't think how many times I've had the opportunity to do it, but have been too petrified of my ears bleeding and my head exploding! Thanks to my travel buddy Sara for convincing me to give it a go. Totally worth it!

a Don't blame you for chickening out. I could never do it.
b Good luck – I'm absolutely sure you'll have a great time!
c How many times have I said you'd love it?

Language note

In informal writing, it is common to omit the subject of the sentence. Sometimes, the verb 'be' is also omitted, even if it is in the past tense. As you read, it is useful to think about what these missing words might be, so that you understand *who* did the action and *when*.

2 Choose the correct meaning for the following words.

1 bar   **a** plus   **b** except

2 drenched   **a** wet   **b** excited

3 whizzing   **a** raining   **b** moving fast

4 courage   **a** fear   **b** bravery

5 petrified   **a** excited   **b** scared

3 Choose the correct verb from the text to complete the sentences. You may need to change the form of the verb.

1 Things rarely .... according to plan when you're hiking, even if you plan your route thoroughly.

2 After 17 years of family holidays at home, we finally .... up the courage to broaden our horizons abroad.

3 I was nervous about scuba diving, but I didn't want to .... out in front of my friends.

4 Just two minutes into the cycle ride, the heavens ....

5 It was my uncle who got me into water-skiing. I .... it a go about seven years ago and have been hooked ever since.

6 The wave took me completely unawares. I .... up underwater, under the boat, with no air.

4 Choose the correct word or phrase for each gap from the list below.

Now I've left the **1** .... of Bangkok, and I'm off on the next **2** ....

of my Asia trip – heading to the Mekong Delta. Looking forward to getting off the

3 .... track! Can't wait to start my volunteering project; I think it'll be a great

way to **4** .... myself in the local culture. But after six weeks in a school, I think I'll

be ready to **5** .... the beach and soak up some rays!

1   **a** hustle and bustle   **b** flotsam and jetsam   **c** hue and cry   **d** ins and outs

2   **a** arm   **b** limb   **c** leg   **d** spine

3   **a** beaten   **b** worn   **c** busy   **d** trodden

4   **a** attend   **b** engage   **c** occupy   **d** immerse

5   **a** grab   **b** beat   **c** hit   **d** knock

B   A travel blog

The Life of a Permanent Nomad

WANDERING EARL.com

Home   About   Wander Fund   Blog   Travel Resources   Links   Tours   Contact Me   Archives   Type and enter to search

Home » Blog » Tales Of A Bollywood Actor

Tales Of A Bollywood Actor
Posted on March 27 by Wandering Earl 8 a.m.

1 | The time was 8 a.m. I had exactly one hour to kill before having to hail a taxi to the airport in order to pick up my close friend who was flying in from Thailand.

2 | Why I had chosen the most ultra-budget, grimiest of hotels in Mumbai was beyond me, but there was nothing I could do at this point but to accept the consequences.

3 | Eventually, the hour did pass and I stood up to finally leave. But just before I reached the door, I noticed a paper calendar taped to the wall. It was a most ordinary calendar, yet something struck me as odd. The date read "February 29th" yet my friend was arriving on March 1st. I suddenly realized that I had forgotten it was a leap year.

4 | Therefore, I had one more day on my own in Mumbai.

5 | I sat back down again in the cafe with my face in my hands, trying to decide how to spend that day, when the man from the reception 'desk' (which was actually just a three-legged wooden chair) approached me. He asked if something was wrong and I proceeded to explain my story.

6 | He listened intently and when I finished, I just expected him to shrug his shoulders, let out a chuckle and wag his head back and forth.

7 | What I absolutely didn't expect him to do was to offer me **an acting role in a BOLLYWOOD TELEVISION SERIES!** (For those who are not as addicted to India as I am, Bollywood is the Indian equivalent of Hollywood.)

8 | At first I thought it was a joke, but without even waiting for my answer, the man returned to the reception chair, made a quick phone call and then informed me that someone would be picking me up from the hotel in thirty minutes.

9 | When I tried to press him for further details, all he said was, "You go and be actor somewhere, I think they will pay you."

JUST ANOTHER DAY ON THE SET

10 | The journey out to Juhu Beach (an upscale, coastal neighborhood of Mumbai) required two taxis, a commuter train and a rickshaw, but the young man who had collected me from the hotel seemed to know exactly where we were headed.

11   We eventually arrived at the set of the Indian soap opera Sansaar, which was actually a beachfront mansion in which half of the inside had been temporarily transformed into a London apartment building. As soon as we entered the door we encountered dozens of people – actors, producers, directors, set techs, errand-boys, etc. – as well as an endless sea of cameras, computers, props and sets. And while this is exactly what one might expect to find in such a place, it all seemed more overwhelming than the wildly chaotic streets outside.

12   I was quickly introduced to the casting director, a young friendly guy who led me into a small living room for a quick chat. After explaining to him that I had absolutely no acting skills whatsoever and was completely uncomfortable in front of a video camera, he promptly offered me a speaking role as a British police officer, a role that required me to act in five different scenes and memorize a page of lines.

13   After a lavish buffet lunch on one of the mansion's terraces overlooking the ocean, where I spent an hour chatting with several of the actors and actresses and trying to memorize my lines, I was handed a British police officer's uniform and directed to my 'changing room', which was actually a closet that didn't even have a door.

14   Then, fighting off my nerves, I walked onto the set and silently prayed to the statue of Ganesh in the corner. As if he magically answered my prayers, I found myself, over the following hour and a half, rising from an absolute nobody to an award-worthy actor. Sure, each scene took at least ten takes due to my mumbling and bumbling, but I think it was quite clear to everyone that it was the passion I showed for my role, not a lack of ability, that was the real culprit.

15   And while the look on my fellow actors' faces, who were playing a family whose daughter was just in a car accident, often appeared to be that of frustration as I repeatedly blurted out, take after take, "I found and sweater, wallet this and car daughter book", there were only looks of pure joy (and perhaps relief) when I finally nailed it and informed them that, "I found this sweater, this wallet and this book in your daughter's car."

16   I'm not exactly sure if joy was what they were supposed to display at that exact moment ... but who am I to say what's right? I'm only an actor, not a director.

17   When the actual director did finally yell out 'CUT!' for the last time, my day of acting did abruptly come to an end. Of course, I went around the room and accepted the handshakes of the other actors and crew, all of whom I assume felt so proud to have worked with me.

18   The young man who had picked me up from my hotel earlier that morning appeared again in order to take me back. But before we left, just as the man at the reception desk had predicted, the casting director handed me 1000 Rupees ($22 USD) and thanked me for my services.

19   Barely able to control my excitement, I left that mansion seriously pondering a new career.

1 Skim read Earl's travel blog. What is it about?

  a Earl compares the real Mumbai to the Mumbai shown in film and TV.

  b Earl meets an Indian movie star while travelling in Mumbai.

  c While in Mumbai, Earl gets the opportunity to act in a TV show.

2 Read Earl's blog and choose the best answer to complete the sentences.

  1 The story began in …

   a an airport lounge.   **b** a hotel reception.

  2 On seeing the calendar, Earl realized that …

   a he had got today's date wrong.   **b** he had got his friend's arrival date wrong.

  3 Earl … the man at reception to contact the TV company.

   a had to persuade   **b** didn't have to persuade

  4 The film set was in a … part of Mumbai.

   a wealthy   **b** poor

  5 The casting director … Earl's acting experience and ability.

   a gave careful consideration to   **b** took no notice of

  6 Earl's acting skills were …

   a better than expected.   **b** terrible.

3 Read the travel blog again and answer the following questions.

  1 Why is the word 'desk' (paragraph 5) written in inverted commas?

  ....

  2 What kind of TV show did Earl perform in?

  ....

  3 What adjective does Earl use to describe the film set?

  ....

  4 What reason does Earl give for his poor acting?

  ....

  5 Why did Earl consider the actors' reaction to his lines inappropriate?

  ....

Language note

Conjunctions are important as they show the relationship between two parts of a sentence. In English, the relationship is sometimes confusing, as some conjunctions have more than one meaning.

yet	a) until the present time	*We haven't received the documents **yet**.*
	b) but / however	*It was a great festival, and **yet** I didn't enjoy it.*
while	a) although	***While** I like London a lot, I wouldn't like to live there.*
	b) at the same time as	*Can you wash up **while** I make dinner?*

4 Find words or phrases in the travel blog with the meanings below.

1 dirtiest (paragraph 2)

2 seemed strange to me (4 words, paragraph 3)

3 shake from side to side (paragraph 6)

4 urge (someone) to give you more information (5 words, paragraph 9)

5 at all (paragraph 12)

6 luxurious (paragraph 13)

7 said suddenly, without thinking (2 words, paragraph 15)

8 get something right (2 words, paragraph 15)

5 'While' and 'yet' are each used twice in Earl's blog (paragraphs 3, 11 and 15). Read the Language note on page 60 and decide whether meaning a or b is correct for the words in bold.

1 I noticed a paper calendar taped to the wall. It was a most ordinary calendar, **yet** something struck me as odd. ......

2 The date read "February 29th" **yet** my friend was arriving on March 1st. ......

3 And **while** this is exactly what one might expect to find in such a place, it all seemed more overwhelming than the wildly chaotic streets outside. ......

4 And **while** the look on my fellow actors' faces [...] often appeared to be that of frustration [...] there were only looks of pure joy [...] when I finally nailed it. ......

Reading tip

Sarcasm is a feature of some humorous or informal texts. Sarcasm is speech or writing which actually means the opposite of what it seems to say. Sarcasm is usually intended to mock or insult someone. You can identify sarcasm when a sentence contradicts what the author is saying in the rest of the text.

6 Would Earl agree with the following statements?

1 He didn't expect the receptionist to be sympathetic and helpful.

2 The film set was well-equipped and well-staffed.

3 The actors were treated extravagantly in every way.

4 The Indian actors were proud to have worked with him.

5 He was excited to have earned so much money that day.

6 He doesn't plan to act in any more Bollywood films.

Next steps

Read more of Earl's Adventures at **www.wanderingearl.com**. How long has Earl been travelling for? Where is he now?

Sign up to **www.blogloving.com** to get updates from the blogs you follow. Why not follow some blogs in English on subjects that interest you?

13 NEWS REPORTS
Newspaper articles

Getting started

1 Do you read the news online, on a phone or in a newspaper?
2 What kind of stories do you prefer to read?
3 What natural disasters have you read about recently?

A   News reports

1 Skim the two reports of a tornado in the USA and find out the information below.

a the day and time of the tornado

b the strength and speed of the tornado

c the location (suburb and town)

d the number of fatalities and injured people

Mile-wide tornado hits Oklahoma

1 A monstrous tornado up to a mile wide roared through the Oklahoma City suburbs, flattening entire neighbourhoods with winds up to 200mph, setting buildings on fire and landing a direct blow on a school.

2 The storm laid waste to scores of buildings in Moore, south of the city. Street after street of the community lay in ruins, with heaps of debris piled up where homes used to be. Cars and lorries were left crumpled on the roadside.

3 The National Weather Service issued an initial finding that the tornado was an EF-4 on the enhanced Fujita scale, the second most-powerful type of twister.

4 In video of the storm, the dark funnel cloud could be seen marching slowly across the green landscape. As it churned through the community, the twister scattered shards of wood, pieces of insulation, awnings, shingles and glass all over the streets.

5 Volunteers and first responders raced to search the debris for survivors.

6 At Plaza Towers Elementary School, the storm tore off the roof, knocked down walls and turned the playground into a mass of [1](**twisting / twisted**) plastic and metal. Several children were pulled alive from the rubble. Rescue workers passed the survivors down a human chain to a triage centre in the car park.

7 The same suburb was hit hard by a tornado in 1999. That storm had the distinction of producing the highest winds recorded near the earth's surface – 302mph.

From: *The Daily Express*
Tuesday 21ˢᵗ May 2013

Oklahoma tornado:
The storm was a monster – even for Tornado Alley

1 Residents of Moore are used to severe weather patterns – but the strength of Monday's twister left them shocked and awed.

2 The people of Moore know a twister when they see one. On 3 May 1999, an EF-5 storm tore through the Oklahoma suburb, killing 36 people and injuring 583. So when a dark, [2](**spinning / spun**) cloud appeared in the skies to the southwest on Monday afternoon, they were prepared - or so they thought. The tornado touched down at 2.46pm.

3 Lando Hite, an exercise rider and caretaker at the Celestial Acres horse training facility, had been readying to weather a regular storm when he realised what was coming. His experience of living in Oklahoma's "Tornado Alley", he said, had likely saved his life: when the wind seemed to die down suddenly, he knew danger was imminent, and took refuge in a stable.

4 "I jumped into one of the [horse] stalls and they collapsed on top of me," Hite, still shirtless and caked in mud, told local news station KFOR later. "It was unbearably loud. You could see stuff [3](**flew / flying**) everywhere, just like in the movie Twister."

5 While the storm wreaked havoc on Celestial Acres, across town in the Warren Theatre's IMAX auditorium, 25-year-old James Dock was sitting down to watch *Star Trek: Into Darkness*. As the movie began, its noisy sound effects were joined by the sound of something heavy [4](**bouncing / bounced**) off the roof of the cinema. "I thought it was hail," Dock told *The Los Angeles Times*. Just before 3pm, the manager came into the theatre and asked patrons to retreat to the hallway for shelter.

6 By that time, the tornado had crossed the nearby Newcastle neighbourhood, and been upgraded to a category EF-4 storm, with wind speeds of 200mph or more. Elderly Moore resident Barbara Garcia was sitting on a stool in her bathroom, hugging her dog as the twister struck. The lights went out, and she felt the stool rise up off the floor. When she came to, she was covered in debris, lying beside an [5](**upturned / upturning**) stove in the rubble of her home. "I hollered for my little dog, and he didn't answer," she said.

7 As the twister bore down on Briarwood Elementary School, pupils took cover under stairs, desks and bathroom sinks. Teachers shielded the children; one lay on top of her own son to protect him from [6](**falling / fallen**) debris. The wind peeled the walls and roof from the building but, remarkably, no one was killed. Plaza Towers Elementary, struck minutes later, was not so lucky. Though some older pupils had been evacuated to a nearby church, those from kindergarten to third grade were still huddled in the building as it succumbed to the storm. [7](**Trapping / Trapped**) in the basement as the water pipes burst, seven children were found drowned beneath the rubble of the school on Monday evening.

8 By Tuesday morning, the death toll was estimated at 24, with further fatalities feared. More than 140 people had been injured. There was a glimmer of hope for Barbara Garcia, who found her dog in the rubble during an on-camera interview with CBS News, apparently uninjured. "Well I got God to answer one prayer to let me be OK," said an emotional Garcia, "but he answered both of them because this was my second prayer."

From: *The Independent*
Tuesday 21st May 2013

② Read the two articles on pages 62–63 and answer the questions below.

1 Identify four buildings mentioned in the texts which were affected by the storm. In which building were there most fatalities?

2 Identify three people who were interviewed for the news reports. Who was knocked out by the tornado?

3 What was Barbara Garcia's 'second prayer'?

Language note – participle adjectives

Present participle adjectives (verb + *ing*) describe what is happening at present.

*In a video of the storm, ... the dark funnel cloud could be seen **marching** slowly across the green landscape.*

Past participle adjectives describe how something was affected in the past.

*Cars and lorries were left **crumpled** on the roadside.*

Participle adjectives can be used before nouns or after verbs such as *be, see, look* or *leave*. They can also start sentences.

③ Look back at the participle adjectives (in brackets) in the two articles. Choose the adjectives that are correct.

④ Vocabulary from these articles may be found in many disaster reports. Match the highlighted vocabulary to its meaning.

1	debris / rubble	a	number of people dead
2	first responder	b	medically trained volunteer
3	triage	c	an emergency medical unit
4	havoc	d	chaos
5	death toll	e	people killed
6	fatalities	f	broken stone and bricks

B   Journalistic styles

① To avoid making their writing sound repetitive, journalists use synonyms for the subjects of their texts. Can you find five words in the article that mean 'tornado'?

....

② A number of words in the reports describe the movement and actions of the tornado. Try to find at least five words.

....

3 Some verbs create an emotive impact by having a strong visual, emotional or auditory component. Complete the sentences below with a verb from the box. You will not need one of them.

flatten	roar	appear	march

1 The verb .... compares the tornado to an unstoppable army.
2 The verb .... is onomatopoeic, that is, the sound of the word is the same as its meaning.
3 The verb .... is visually strong, and helps the reader to picture the scene.

4 Which report do you think is more emotive? Why do you think so?

Reading tip

No two newspapers report events in the same way. Newspapers are written to appeal to a certain readership. Journalists tailor articles towards different genders, ages, levels of education and political views. It is worth knowing the general readership of a newspaper before reading articles, as it often affects the content and style!

5 Compare the styles of the two articles and put a tick in the correct column.

	The Independent	The Daily Express	Both articles
1 Which article is organized in chronological order?			
2 Which article has shorter paragraphs?			
3 Which article is more emotive?			
4 Which article is more detailed?			

6 What age, gender, and number of people do you think read *The Independent* and *The Daily Express*? Write down a guess then check your answer in the key.

Next steps

Read about the Oklahoma tornado in other newspapers. You can find these by searching online for "May 2013 Moore tornado". How do the articles compare to the articles printed here in terms of length, factual content, emotional content and emotive language?

Note down any new vocabulary connected with natural disasters. Pay attention to vocabulary used in more than one article as more frequent words and phrases are more useful to learn.

FORMAL DISCUSSION
Academic essays and journals

Getting started

1 Is climate change often in the news in your country?
2 What negative effects of climate change have you read about?
3 Have you read about any positive effects of climate change?

A Academic essays

  Skim this academic essay. What question does it answer?

  a What is the case against the theory that humans cause climate change?
  b What are the causes and effects of global warming?
  c What are the best theories that explain climate change?

Environmental policies worldwide aim to convince us to reduce our carbon footprint in order to reduce the threat of climate change. However, many scientists doubt whether the greenhouse gases released by human activity really do cause global warming.

The global climate is undoubtedly changing. Since the earth formed an estimated 4,600 million years ago, it has alternated between being a frozen planet and a steaming hothouse. **(A)....** Environmentalists claim that today's rising temperatures result from our increased use of greenhouse gases. **(B)....** They play a vital role in making our planet habitable. Sunlight reaching the Earth's surface radiates back into the atmosphere as heat, which is absorbed by the greenhouse gases and re-radiated to Earth, warming the planet and allowing life on Earth to exist.**1**(However / Subsequently), environmentalists argue that the burning of fossil fuels is increasing the concentration of atmospheric greenhouse gases, which in turn is increasing global temperatures. By reducing fuel consumption, they believe global warming may be reversed.

To what extent, however, is this true? Certainly carbon dioxide levels are rising. **(C)....** If environmentalists are right, temperatures should have risen accordingly. **2**(Although / Yet) the timing does not appear to coincide. **(D)....** Scientists **3**(also / thus) question whether higher levels of greenhouse gases drive the warming at all, and suggest that warm temperatures cause carbon dioxide levels to rise, not vice versa. **4**(Moreover / Despite this), the theory cannot account for the levels of atmospheric carbon dioxide 8 to 20 times their current values during the Ordovician Ice Age 500 million years ago.

Attempts to reduce carbon levels are undoubtedly sensible. The burning of fossil fuels pollutes the environment, causing breathing difficulties and affecting biodiversity. **(E)....** **5**(Nonetheless / Consequently), the notion that this causes global warming is seen by many as ridiculous.

2 The chart below shows an Enviromentalist's view of global warming. Read the academic essay closely and add verbs from the text. In some cases more than one word is possible.

Sunlight **1** .... from the earth into the atmosphere in the form of heat.

↓

Greenhouse gases in the atmosphere **2** .... the heat.

↓

The heat is **3** .... back to Earth.

↓

The concentration of greenhouse gases increases when fossil fuels are **4** ....

↓

This causes global temperatures to **5** ....

↓

It may be possible to **6** .... global warming by decreasing the use of fossil fuels.

Reading tip

Cohesive devices link sentences and paragraphs together. An understanding of these will help you follow a writer's argument.

Topic sentences show the main idea of a paragraph. They may also show how this paragraph relates to preceding paragraphs. **Link words** show the relationship between two sentences. They commonly show addition, contrast, cause or effect.

3 Find the correct places for extracts 1–5 in the essay.

1 Pre-industrial levels were around 285 parts per million (ppm); they stood at about 315 ppm in 1960, and current levels are about 390 ppm.

2 These include water vapour, carbon dioxide, ozone and to a lesser extent chlorofluorocarbons, nitrous oxide and sulphur dioxide.

3 Researchers Singer and Avery (2007) observed that temperatures should have risen steadily since the industrial boom of the 1940s, but instead they dropped for three decades.

4 Since human civilisation emerged 20,000 years ago, average global temperatures have oscillated between 12°C and 22°C. In the last century, they warmed by about 0.5°C.

5 Furthermore, declining fuel stocks in an ever more industrialised planet make it more necessary than ever to be prudent with our resources.

4 Read the essay again and choose the best link words in brackets.

Skim read the article. Do Donahue and his team believe that climate change is always negative?

The green flip side to carbon emissions

Fred Pearce

1   The planet is getting lusher, and we are responsible. Carbon dioxide generated by human activity is stimulating photosynthesis and causing a beneficial greening of the Earth's surface.

2   For the first time, researchers claim to have shown that the increase in plant cover is due to this "CO_2 fertilisation effect" rather than other causes. However, it remains unclear whether the effect can counter any negative consequences of global warming, such as the spread of deserts.

3   Recent satellite studies have shown that the planet is harbouring more vegetation overall, but pinning down the cause has been difficult. Factors such as higher temperatures, extra rainfall, and an increase in atmospheric CO_2 – which helps plants use water more efficiently – could all be boosting vegetation.

4   To home in on the effect of CO_2, Randall Donohue of Australia's national research institute, the CSIRO in Canberra, monitored vegetation at the edges of deserts in Australia, southern Africa, the US Southwest, North Africa, the Middle East and central Asia. These are regions where there is ample warmth and sunlight, but only just enough rainfall for vegetation to grow, so any change in plant cover must be the result of a change in rainfall patterns or CO_2 levels, or both.

5   If CO_2 levels were constant, then the amount of vegetation per unit of rainfall ought to be constant, too. However, the team found that this figure rose by 11 per cent in these areas between 1982 and 2010, mirroring the rise in CO_2 (Geophysical Research Letters, doi.org/mqx). Donohue says this lends "strong support" to the idea that CO_2 fertilisation drove the greening.

6   Climate change studies have predicted that many dry areas will get drier and that some deserts will expand. Donohue's findings make this less certain.

7   However, the greening effect may not apply to the world's driest regions. Beth Newingham of the University of Idaho, Moscow, recently published the result of a 10-year experiment involving a greenhouse set up in the Mojave desert of Nevada. She found "no sustained increase in biomass" when extra CO_2 was pumped into the greenhouse. "You cannot assume that all these deserts are the same," she says. "Enough water needs to be present for the plants to respond at all."

8   The extra plant growth could have knock-on effects on climate, Donohue says, by increasing rainfall, affecting river flows and changing the likelihood of wildfires. It will also absorb more CO_2 from the air, potentially damping down global warming but also limiting the CO_2 fertilisation itself.

9   Donohue cannot yet say to what extent CO_2 fertilisation will affect vegetation in the coming decades. But if it proves to be significant, the future may be much greener and more benevolent than many climate modellers predict.

From: *The New Scientist*

2 Read the article in detail and choose the correct answer.

1 Donahue and his team have claimed that …

   a there is increased vegetation at desert margins.

   b increased vegetation results from increased CO_2.

   c CO_2 is one of several factors which is increasing vegetation.

2 Desert margins were chosen for the study because …

   a there is very little human interference there.

   b water and CO_2 are the only limiting factors.

   c they are sunny and warm.

3 According to the research, the level of vegetation in these areas …

   a increased at the same rate as atmospheric CO_2.

   b remained constant from 1982 to 2010.

   c rose by 11 per cent per year between 1982 and 2010.

4 Beth Newingham …

   a disagrees that atmospheric CO_2 can increase vegetation.

   b believes that some regions are too dry for CO_2 fertilisation.

   c doubts the results of Donahue's experiment.

Language note

Authors sometimes use hedging language to express their view on a subject, and when reading reports it is useful to be able to separate fact from fiction. When reading reports of claims, it is useful to be able to separate facts from conjecture. Facts use phrases like *undoubtedly* and *it is evident*, or are written simply without modal verbs. Hedging language is used to describe beliefs, opinions and conjecture. It includes modal verbs like *can, could* and *may*, or verbs like *claim, predict* or *argue*.

3 Are the following statements reported as fact, or in hedging language?

1 Humans are responsible for making the planet greener. (paragraph 1)

2 The increase in vegetation is due to higher temperatures, increased rainfall and the effect of CO_2 fertilisation. (paragraph 3)

3 The increase in vegetation in Donahue's study resulted from CO_2 fertilisation. (paragraph 5)

4 Deserts will not get drier as a result of climate change. (paragraph 6)

5 Earth will be greener in the future. (paragraph 9)

4 Highlight hedging language in the text.

Next steps

Find some other stories about climate change at **www.newscientist.com**. What do scientists believe about climate change?

15 OPINION PIECES
A newspaper column

Getting started

1 Have you read any newspaper stories about new cures for health problems?
2 Where can you read the best advice on health care?
3 How do you know this is the best advice?

A Opinion columns

1 Before you read, match the vocabulary to its meaning.

1	acupuncture	a	words intended to stop someone feeling worried
2	reassurance	b	a fake pill or treatment that the recipient believes is real
3	trial	c	staying in bed on medical advice
4	placebo	d	inserting fluid into the body using a syringe
5	ritual	e	medicine that reduces swelling
6	injection	f	a treatment involving inserting needles under the skin
7	anti-inflammatory drug	g	an experiment to test how effective something is
8	bed rest	h	a series of actions performed in a certain order

2 Which of the items in Exercise 1 do you think could help reduce back pain?

3 Skim read the opinion column. What is the purpose of the article?

a to highlight the problems with acupuncture
b to argue that a trial was badly conducted
c to criticize the culture of pill taking
d to encourage doctors to prescribe placebos

4 Identify the topics of paragraphs 2–9. Write the paragraph numbers in the spaces.

1 suggested reasons for the results ....
2 education – a better cure than medication ....
3 the results of the study ....
4 the culture of medication as treatment ....
5 how a study was carried out ....
6 the definition of a key word in this article ....
7 the causes of back pain ....
8 the effects of various back pain treatments ....

Medicalisation – don't take it lying down

September 29th

Ben Goldacre

1 This week a major new study was published on acupuncture. Many newspapers said it showed acupuncture performing better than medical treatment: in fact it was 8 million times more interesting than that.

2 They took 1162 patients who had suffered with back pain for an average of 8 years (so these were patients who had failed with medical treatment anyway) and divided them into 3 groups. The first group simply had some more medical treatment; the second group had full-on acupuncture with all the trimmings, the needles all put carefully into the correct "meridians" in accordance with ancient Chinese stuff, and so on; while the third group just had some bloke pretending to be an acupuncturist, sticking needles in their skin at random. The study set a threshold for "response to treatment", which was an improvement of 33% on 3 items out of a bigger scale, or 12% on one symptom scale. So this was not "getting better", or a "cure".

3 And what were the results? Firstly, 27% of the medical treatment group improved: this is an impressive testament to the well known healing power of simply "being in a trial", since medical treatment hadn't helped these patients for the preceding 8 years. Meanwhile 47% of the acupuncture group improved, but the sting is this: 44% of the fake acupuncture group improved too. There was no statistically significant difference between proper, genuine ancient wisdom acupuncture, and fake, "bung a needle in, anywhere you fancy, with a bit of theatrical ceremony" acupuncture.

4 There are three possible explanations for this finding. One is that sticking needles in your body anywhere at random helps back pain due to some physiological mechanism. The second is that theatrical ceremony, reassurance, the thought of someone doing something useful, and a chat with someone nice helps back pain. (The third option is "a bit of both").

5 Now as I have said so many times before, the placebo effect is not about a sugar pill, it's about the cultural meaning of a treatment, and our expectations: we know from research that two sugar pills are more effective than one, that a salt water injection is better for pain than a sugar pill, that colour and packaging have a beneficial effect, and so on. Interestingly, there has even been a trial on patients with arm pain specifically comparing a placebo pill against a placebo ritual involving a sham medical device, modelled on acupuncture, which found that the elaborate ritual was more effective than the simple sugar pill. "Placebo" is not a unitary phenomenon, there is not "one type of placebo".

6 But the most important background information missing from the news reports wasn't about the details of the study: it was about back pain. Because back pain isn't like epilepsy or tuberculosis. Most of the big risk factors for a niggle turning into chronic longstanding back pain are personal, psychological, and social: things like depression, job dissatisfaction, unavailability of light duty on return to work, and so on.

7 And the evidence on treatments tells an even more interesting psychosocial story: sure, anti-inflammatory drugs are better than placebo. But more than that, bed rest is actively harmful, specific exercises can be too, and proper trial data shows that simply giving advice to "stay active" speeds recovery, reduces chronic disability, and reduces time off work.

8 We don't like stories and solutions like that for our health problems. There are huge industries telling you that your tiredness is due to some "chromium deficiency" (buy the pill); your cloudy headed foggy feeling can be fixed with vitamin pills, pills, and more pills. It is a brave doctor who dares to bring up psychosocial issues for any complaint when a patient has been consistently told it is biomedical by every newspaper, every magazine, and every quack in town.

9 But in conditions like back pain or fatigue, information alone can make a difference to the suffering of millions. In Australia, a simple public information campaign ("Back Pain: don't take it lying down", arf) was shown to reduce back pain significantly in the whole population. Meanwhile journalists, patients, quacks, politicians and editors would all rather talk about magical, technical pills and rituals.

From: *The Guardian*

5 How is this text structured?

1 The writer makes his main point at the beginning of the article, and the following paragraphs support his argument.

2 A series of arguments lead the reader towards the writer's main point at the end of the article.

6 The writer leads the reader from one point to the next by linking paragraphs by a single topic. Which two paragraphs ...

1 examine the results of the experiment? .... and ....

2 describe the health benefits of fake treatments? .... and ....

3 describe the factors that make back pain worse? .... and ....

4 describe treatments that are considered unpopular? .... and ....

7 Once you have understood the structure of the text, you can locate information more easily. Read the column in detail and choose the correct answers.

1 The patients in the trial

   a had all suffered from back pain for at least eight years.

   b all received acupuncture treatment.

   c all continued taking medicine.

   d received one of three possible treatments.

2 According to the author, the reason for the improvement among those receiving medical treatment was ...

   a a mystery.

   b because they were participating in an experiment.

   c because they were taking different drugs from before.

   d because they took the drugs for more than eight years.

3 Statistically, the experiment showed that ...

   a acupuncture is the best cure for back pain.

   b real acupuncture is no better than sham acupuncture.

   c acupuncture does more harm than good.

   d medical treatment is more effective if used together with acupuncture.

4 The results imply that ...... can improve back pain.

   a doing nothing

   b an understanding of how acupuncture works

   c receiving positive, personal attention

   d taking more than one treatment

5 The author observes that ...

   a some placebos work better than others.

   b sugar pills are the most effective placebo.

   c it is hard to measure the effect of placebos.

   d placebos only work among people of certain ages.

8 Which treatment from Exercise 1 is ineffective at improving back pain, according to the article?

B Vocabulary and style

1 Re-read paragraph 2 and the Reading tip below. Do you think the style of this article is formal or informal?

Reading tip

formal texts
- avoid use of personal pronouns
- are objective, not subjective
- use standard punctuation

informal texts
- use personal pronouns
- use idioms and less formal vocabulary, such as phrasal verbs
- use more varied punctuation, such as brackets, question marks and exclamation marks

---

2 Find the informal words and phrases from paragraph 2 with the following meanings.

1 complete = f........ – o........
2 with special extra details = with a........ t........ t........
3 practices, beliefs and traditions = s........
4 man = b........
5 inserting = s........

3 Re-read the text. What other features indicate an informal style?

4 Why do you think the author adopts an informal style?

1 A formal style is not suitable for this subject matter.
2 He wants to make his argument more accessible to readers.
3 He lacks the education to write in a formal way.

5 The author maintains his authority by referring to research that supports his argument. Highlight three pieces of research mentioned in the text.

6 The author uses precise, technical vocabulary to show his understanding of these subjects. Find at least five vocabulary items related to each of the following topics.

a health   b research

Next steps

Find this article at **www.badscience.net**. Read the comments left by readers. Do they tend to agree or disagree with Ben Goldacre's opinion?

What other issues does he discuss?

16 TEXTBOOKS
Fact-filled educational articles

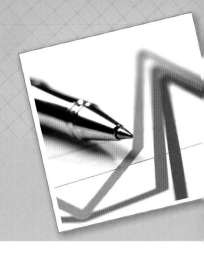

Getting started

1 Have you ever used an English textbook to study another subject?
2 In what ways do textbooks present information?
3 How do textbooks prepare students for exams?

A Urbanization

1 Read this extract from a geography textbook. What is the main purpose of this passage?

   a to exemplify how the world is becoming increasingly urbanized

   b to describe the causes of increased urbanization

   c to outline some of the main problems caused by urbanization

   d to compare urban areas in developed and less developed countries

Urbanization

For the first time in history, more than half of the world's population of 7 billion are city-dwellers. Over the next 20 years, this figure is expected to rise by a further two billion. Expansion is particularly large in less developed countries where there are an estimated 70 million new urban residents every year. In the world's two poorest regions, South Asia and Sub-Saharan Africa, the urban population is predicted to double by 2030.

> There are three reasons for the rising figures:
> 1 rural-to-urban migration
> 2 the natural population increase within cities
> 3 the reclassification of rural areas into urban ones, as villages develop into towns, or are swallowed up by urban sprawl.

Such growth is inevitable, as no country has developed without going through urbanization and industrialization. Indeed, around 70% of global GDP is generated in cities. However, rapid uncontrolled urbanization tends to result in huge populations living in slums. In fact, around one third of the world's urban population are slum-dwellers – currently over 900 million people. Although an estimated 227 million people in the developing world were lifted out of slum conditions between 2000 and 2010, primarily in China and India, the number of slum dwellers continues to increase by six million every year.

2 Put a tick in the correct column.

	True	False
1 Urbanization is more evident in developing countries.	....	....
2 The main reason for increasing urban populations is migration.	....	....
3 All developed countries have high urban populations.	....	....
4 There are six million new slum dwellers in India and China per year.	....	....

3 Complete the glossary below with terms from the text.

.... the movement of people from the countryside to the cities

.... population growth due to changes in birth and death rates

.... the growth of cities into surrounding settlements

.... a substantial increase in output from factories and businesses

.... an overcrowded area of a city with substandard living conditions

4 Which of the figures below incorrectly illustrates the information in the text?

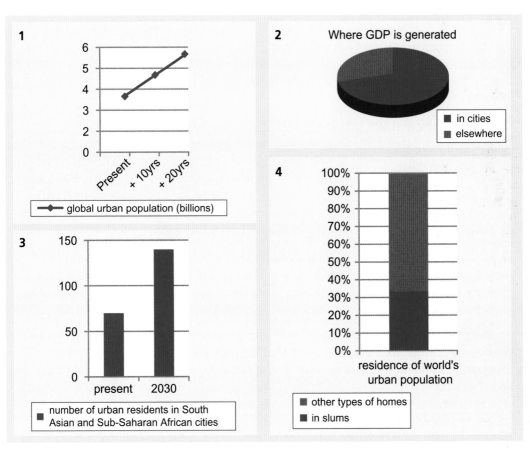

1 global urban population (billions)

2 Where GDP is generated — in cities / elsewhere

3 number of urban residents in South Asian and Sub-Saharan African cities — present / 2030

4 residence of world's urban population — other types of homes / in slums

B   Urban poverty

1 Textbooks often use photographs to illustrate facts in the text. Read the text below about urban poverty in the UK, and choose the best photograph to illustrate paragraphs 1, 2 and 4. You will not need them all.

paragraph 1: ....   paragraph 2: ....   paragraph 4: ....

a

b

c

d

e

1 In the UK, poverty tends to be centred in inner cities. These areas were the site of heavy industry in the late 1800s and early 1900s, and factory workers would reside in low-cost housing nearby, typically rows of small terraced houses. By the mid 20th century, many of the factories had closed down, and the houses were run down and lacked modern amenities, such as indoor plumbing and electricity.

2 In the 1950s and 60s, **urban regeneration** schemes were put in place to improve living standards. Old terraces were knocked down and replaced with modern buildings, chiefly tower blocks, giving occupants access to basic hot water, electricity and sewerage systems. However, they were poorly built and soon required costly repairs. Meanwhile, the social problems associated with poverty were not addressed, and the inner city tower blocks became vandalised, graffiti-ridden and renowned for crime and social tension.

3 In the 1980s, riots in several impoverished British cities led to a number of **urban renewal schemes**. An example is the London Docklands. Over the past twenty years a number of initiatives have been put into place to improve and rejuvenate the area.

4 Gentrification has taken place, with old industrial warehouses being refurbished to create luxury apartments that attract young professionals, who boost the local economy by paying taxes and spending money. Transport links have also been improved, including the extension of rail and underground routes and the construction of City Airport. New business has been encouraged through low rates and rents. Although the scheme is considered a success, some original residents complain that the influx of middle class professionals has altered the character of the area. Moreover, such schemes cannot be implemented everywhere due to the huge costs, and fears that investors may not see a return in their investments for a long time, if ever.

Reading tip

Even though technical terms are sometimes not covered in ordinary dictionaries, you can often find explanations in the text nearby. Look closely in surrounding sentences and see if a definition is actually provided in the way the subject is discussed.

2 Use the text to write your own definitions of the following terms.

1 urban regeneration   2   urban renewal schemes   3   gentrification

3 When learning from a textbook, it is often useful to note down information in a diagrammatic way. Complete the flow chart.

Factory workers lived in **1** ....

↓

These became **2** ....

↓

They were demolished and replaced by **3** ....

↓

These became hotspots for social problems such as **4** ....

↓

In some areas, urban renewal schemes have been initiated, e.g. **5** ....

↓

Improved transport links and housing attracts **6** ....

4 Use the information in the text to complete the table below.

	Advantages	Disadvantages
Urban regeneration	Improves living standards and health; provides basic amenities, e.g. water and electricity	**1**
Urban renewal	**2**	Extremely costly, so not viable in cities unlikely to see a return on investment
Gentrification	Brings in professionals who spend money and pay taxes, thus improving the local economy	**3**

5 Read about urban poverty in Rio de Janeiro. Number the topics below in the order they appear in the text.

problems within shanty towns   ....

solutions to the shanty town problem   ....

an example of an improved slum   ....

the appearance of shanty towns   ....

the location of shanty towns   ....

| Home | Teachers | Interactive | Geotopics | Video |

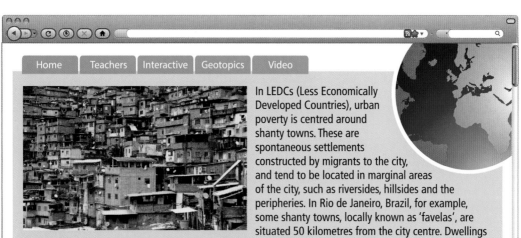

In LEDCs (Less Economically Developed Countries), urban poverty is centred around shanty towns. These are spontaneous settlements constructed by migrants to the city, and tend to be located in marginal areas of the city, such as riversides, hillsides and the peripheries. In Rio de Janeiro, Brazil, for example, some shanty towns, locally known as 'favelas', are situated 50 kilometres from the city centre. Dwellings are constructed using whatever temporary building materials are available to the residents, such as pieces of wood and metal sheeting. There are no sanitation services, electricity or water supplies. Due to overcrowding, diseases spread rapidly, and there are often high levels of crime, violence, drugs and unemployment. Furthermore, because of the precarious locations in which they are positioned, shanty towns are susceptible to natural disasters such as mudslides and flash floods.

Early attempts to clear cities of slum residences have proven ineffective over the years. Clearing an area just leaves a space for new migrants to move into, while rehoming slum dwellers in adequate housing elsewhere is extremely expensive and may even serve to increase the flow of rural migrants to urban areas. Less costly and more effective have been the self-help schemes which grant residents official owner-ship of their land and give them the chance to improve their own living conditions. In Rocinha, one of Rio de Janeiro's largest shanty towns which first developed in the 1950s, authorities provided residents with the building materials they needed to upgrade their makeshift dwellings into permanent, brick and tile homes, often several storeys high, using their own labour. Electricity, paved roads and water pipes have gradually been added using the money saved. Today, Rocinha now has a thriving economy consisting of shops, banks, pharmacies, small industries and even a local TV channel, TV Roc; and with its relatively central, coastal location, it is now quite an attractive neighbourhood.

6 Look back at the texts on pages 76 and 78. Which places do the following sentences refer to? The answer can be *UK*, *Rio de Janeiro*, or *both*.

1 The poorer residents live at the edge of the city.

....

2 At first, authorities used strategies that failed to solve the problem.

....

3 Residents had little choice about how their neighbourhood would develop.

....

4 The government used a relatively inexpensive scheme to reduce urban poverty.

....

Reading tip

When taking notes for an assignment, it is important to analyse whether a text is useful and relevant to the question. To do this, read the assignment question carefully, then skim various texts to decide if they provide you with the information you need.

7 Read the assignment questions below. Which two questions could you answer using the information in this unit?

1 Choose a city which has undergone rapid urbanization. Describe how urbanization has changed the shape and appearance of the city, and examine some of the problems urbanization causes.

2 Choose a settlement where the population is changing due to migration. Give evidence for the migration and explain in detail why it is taking place.

3 For an urban area which is changing, describe the changes taking place and give reasons for the changes. Suggest what problems and opportunities the change has brought to the residents.

8 For each of the questions in Exercise 7, which place would you choose to illustrate your answer, the UK or Rio de Janeiro? Explain why.

9 Choose one of the assignment questions in Exercise 7. Note down which information from the texts you would use to answer each part of the question.

Next steps

Read more about the London Docklands at **www.dockland.co.uk**. What attractions can you visit there?

Read **www.unhabitat.org/stats** for some interesting statistics about cities around the world.

17 CREATIVE DESCRIPTIONS
Poetry

Getting started

1 Have you ever been to Italy?
2 What adjectives do you associate with Italy?
3 Have you read any stories or poems about Italy?

A Poetry

1 Read the poem. What does each verse describe?

a a different meal in Italy
b a different city in Italy
c a different thing that Italy is famous for

2 Complete the table with the things the poet mentions tasting, seeing, hearing, feeling and smelling in each verse.

	Verse 1	Verse 2	Verse 3	Verse 4
Taste	bitter espresso, cheese, bread and fruit	3	lasagne, gnocchi, vino della casa	grappa, vin santo, limoncello, biscotti
See	1	laundry, darting birds, ice blue sky	cobblestones	7
Hear		4	5	8
Feel		cool, fresh air	6	
Smell	2		spices	

Reading tip

When foreign words are added to English texts, they are written in *italics*. In descriptive writing, the use of foreign words helps to makes the description more evocative. There is a glossary for the poem on page 82.

3 The poet aims to convey a different mood in each verse. Which verse would you associate the following adjectives with? You can refer to a verse more than once.

1 bright ....
2 bustling ....
3 breezy ....

4 scented ....
5 noisy ....
6 intimate ....

Italy in One Day
by
Mike Orlock

If I could feed you Italy in one day,
served within a cup for you to savor,
I'd begin in sunny Sorrento
south of Naples,
the morning air perfumed by lemon trees
whose fruit is distilled into the liqueur
that the locals pride themselves in making;
you hold a small espresso cup between
index finger and thumb
and wrinkle your nose at the bitter
flavour of a first tentative sip
between nibbles of cheese and bread
and fruit
in a tiny cafe that overlooks the
Mediterranean
and the hazy outline of the island
of Capri in the distance.

If I could feed you Italy in one day,
pressed between the slices of a
fresh *panini*,
I'd take you to the Tuscan hills
far from the beaten paths of tourists
north of Siena,
the afternoon as fresh as laundry
drying on the lattice of clothesline
of the apartment across the piazza;
women's voices dart like birds overhead,
flying in and out of open windows
as we share bites of our sandwich,
thick with tomato, cheese, and basil
simple ingredients that yield a complexity
of tastes washed down with swallows of
cold *chinotto*
under an ice blue sky.

If I could feed you Italy in one day,
prepared *al forno* like a *primo piatto* of
lasagna or *gnocchi*,

I'd take you to an obscure *osteria* just outside
the *Duomo*
in central Florence,
where the waiters sing you to your table
with operatic theatricality
and the *vino della casa* is the rich ruby colors
of the evening as it settles on the city,
soft as a silk scarf slipping through
your fingers;
we feel the heat of the kitchen
press against the cool of coming night,
our noses florid with the spices of our meals
as we feed each other forkfuls from
our plates;
the streets are alive with the commotion of
traffic
and the banter of voices bouncing like balls
down the cobblestones of the *Via*.

If I could feed you Italy in one day,
poured like dark *grappa* in a delicate
tulip glass,
I'd end at *taverna* in a remote *campo*
in the heart of Venice,
where the tables are draped in checkered
linen
under quiet awnings far from
the chaos of the Grande Canal;
the sweetness of the day lingers
in the echolalia of lapping water
and the sounds of gondoliers at work;
we indulge ourselves in the ablutions
of *vin santo*, *biscotti* dipped in sweet wine,
in *limoncello* or *amaro* sipped
from chilled glasses,
in espresso black
as the Venetian sky at night.
If I could feed you Italy in one day,
would we ever feel the need to eat again?

Glossary of Italian words

al forno – baked in an oven
amaro, grappa, limoncello – Italian liqueurs
biscotti – almond biscuits
campo – square
chinotto – a soft drink made from citrus fruit
Duomo – cathedral
gnocchi – dumplings made of flour and potato
gondolier – a man who steers a *gondola*
(a traditional, narrow boat) on the canals in Venice
lasagne – a pasta dish

osteria – a small restaurant
panini – a type of Italian bread
piazza – town square
primo piatto – first (main) course
of a meal
taverna – small restaurant
Via – street
vin santo – dessert wine
vino della casa – house wine

B Poetic language and devices

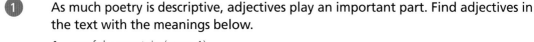

As much poetry is descriptive, adjectives play an important part. Find adjectives in the text with the meanings below.

1 careful, uncertain (verse 1) ....
2 unclear (verse 1) ....
3 well-travelled (verse 2) ....
4 little-known (verse 3) ....
5 elaborate (verse 3) ....

Reading tip

Writers of poetry often use similes (comparing two things by saying A is 'as' or 'like' B) to make their descriptions more vivid. When creating similes, a writer may compare something in a scene with something that is not present.

*Although it was warm, my hands were **as cold as** ice.*

Alternatively the poet may compare two things, both of which are present in the scene.

*Her eyes sparkled **like the diamonds** on her necklace.*

Do you think one way is more effective or more evocative than the other? Could they be used in different circumstances to different effect?

Read the poem to find out what these similes describe.

1 What is 'as fresh as laundry drying on the lattice of clothesline of the apartment across the piazza'?
2 What darts 'like birds overhead, flying in and out of open windows'?
3 What is 'the rich ruby colors of the evening as it settles on the city'?
4 What is 'soft as a silk scarf slipping through your fingers'?
5 What bounces 'like balls down the cobblestones of the *Via*'?
6 What is 'black as the Venetian sky at night'?

3 As well as similes, poets utilize a number of other devices to make their poems pleasant to hear. Which of the following devices is used in 'Italy in One Day'?

1 Alliteration
The repetition of consonant sounds at the beginnings of words.

Example: *Round and round the rugged rock the ragged rascal ran*

2 A regular rhythm
Where stressed and unstressed syllables make a regular pattern throughout.

Example: ● ·· ● · ·● · ● ·
Just for a handful of silver he left us

● ··● ·· ● ·· ●
Just for a riband to stick in his coat
(Robert Browning)

3 Repetition
Where a phrase is repeated several times throughout the poem.

Example: *Half a league, half a league,*
Half a league onward,
All in the valley of Death,
Rode the six hundred.
(Tennyson)

4 Rhyme
Where words have the same final sound.

Example: *Roses are red, violets are blue*
sugar is sweet and so are you.
(Traditional)

Language note

As well as repeating the first line of each verse, the poet also repeats the structure 'the (noun) of (noun)'. This focuses the reader's attention on one particular aspect of a noun, for example, **the** *sweetness* **of the** day.

4 Highlight other examples of 'the … of …' in the poem. How many are there?

Next steps

Why not find other poems by Mike Orlock online? Compare the poetic devices he uses in different poems.

Find poems or novels about your home town, or places you have visited. Does the writer's description match your own feelings and experiences?

18 INTERESTS AND HOBBIES
'How to' guides

Getting started

1 What are your hobbies?

2 Do your hobbies require any special skills or techniques?

3 Where do you read about how to learn or perfect these techniques?

A   Tips from forums

1 One of the more enjoyable aspects of a hobby is meeting like-minded people online and getting useful ideas. Read the explanations below. What hobby does each extract refer to?

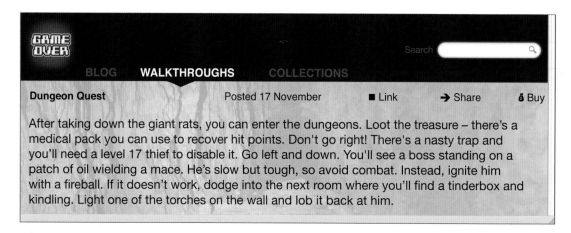

GAME OVER

BLOG   **WALKTHROUGHS**   COLLECTIONS

Search

Dungeon Quest   Posted 17 November   ■ Link   → Share   ᵹ Buy

After taking down the giant rats, you can enter the dungeons. Loot the treasure – there's a medical pack you can use to recover hit points. Don't go right! There's a nasty trap and you'll need a level 17 thief to disable it. Go left and down. You'll see a boss standing on a patch of oil wielding a mace. He's slow but tough, so avoid combat. Instead, ignite him with a fireball. If it doesn't work, dodge into the next room where you'll find a tinderbox and kindling. Light one of the torches on the wall and lob it back at him.

Toby Harding   blues guitarist and historian   Home   Email

Cart 🛒

Performances   Lyrics&MP3s   CDs&DVDs   Media Archives | For Guitarists | Blues Resources

Lessons   Reading   Tab   Instruments and gear | Advanced techniques |

All sorts of things have been used to produce the slide effect, from pocket knives to bones and pipes. The most popular is probably the neck of a broken bottle, although nowadays pre-packaged metal or glass tubes are available from music stores. Metal slides give a better sustain effect, while glass slides have a mellower tone. Slide the tube over a left hand finger, usually the third or fourth. Rest it on the strings, directly over the fret, without pressing down. Glide the slide along to create a continuous change in pitch. It takes practice to perfect the intonation and tone.

Values are the different shades of grey between white and black. An understanding of values is essential when using media such as graphite and charcoal, as it allows you to translate light and shadows into shading and create the illusion of a third dimension on a two dimensional surface. The first step is to identify the light source, the shadows on the object, the shadow cast by the object and the highlights, the brightest of the light values. These are then translated into a range of values. The best way to do this is by squinting. This eliminates details and allows you to see simple values and their shapes. Accentuating light and shadow by using extreme values will produce a striking, dynamic image with high contrast. Low contrast images can appear flat, so it is best to utlize a full range.

2 Which of the following items of advice are given in these pages?
☐ It's not necessary to kill all the giant rats.
☐ Disable the trap before taking the path to the left.
☐ The boss is best defeated from a distance.
☐ The best way to create a slide effect can be made using a broken bottle.
☐ It is more difficult to make a good sound with a metal tube than a glass one.
☐ Use the fingers of both hands on the string to improve the tone.
☐ An object's values can be misrepresented if you squint at it.
☐ A high contrast image will appear more three-dimensional.

Reading tip

Hobbyists often use specialist vocabulary which sometimes native speakers do not recognize. Hobbyist language can sometimes be considered a language in itself! Be selective about the vocabulary you learn. Focus on vocabulary related to your interests, rather than on subjects you are less interested in.

3 Choose one of the texts in Exercise 1 and complete the mind map with useful vocabulary related to the hobby. Can you think of more ways to categorize the vocabulary?

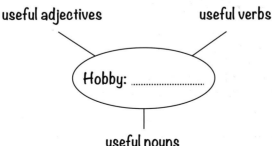

useful adjectives   useful verbs

Hobby: ....

useful nouns

B   An account

1   Reading about peoples' experiences can inspire you to try something new yourself. Read about Michael's experiences making a video game. Which adjective below best describes his attempt?

unsuccessful	enjoyable	frustrating	easy

Michael Rundle 🅟 Follow

GUIDE: How To Make A Video Game In Two Weeks (With No Experience)

Posted: 03/01 16:15 GMT | Updated: 07/01 08:23 GMT

GET UK TECH NEWSLETTERS: [Enter email] [Search]

FOLLOW: Video, Games, construct2, Gamemaker, Gaming, How To Make Video Games, UK Tech News

Two weeks ago I decided to make a video game with no experience. I didn't know what I wanted to make, or how. I pretty much succeeded. Here's how I did it.

1 In the classic manual of how to make video games the first few chapters usually focus on exploring your ideas, playing other games and insisting that you need to know what you're making before you start. This is good advice. But we only had two weeks. So ignore it. For me, the most important first step I took was firing up a modern, entry-level piece of game making software, and seeing what it did. Only when I'd followed a few tutorials, made a little guy move about and realised "hey, I can do this" was I able to have confidence to dream a little bigger. Fortunately there is a ton of great software out there to help you get started.

2 Making my game really started coming together when I had my own character jump, climb and eventually plummet to his death. For a while many game makers will give you the option of using pre-made character art – and there is also no shortage of art to use online – it's when you have something all of your own that you'll start to really enjoy yourself. My character was very simple and easy to draw. Theoretically. While I have some experience as an artist, I still found animating characters surprisingly time consuming until I got into a groove.

3 Making games is like solving a wonderful puzzle – in fact, it's pretty much a game in itself. For instance, I needed to make a ladder for my little guy. Simple right? Not really. That behaviour wasn't built into the software, so I had to invent it. A search on their forums taught me to disable certain types of movement when my guy collided with a ladder tile. A bit of tinkering meant he could go up and down the ladder – but now he did it automatically every time he touched one, meaning he couldn't run past without climbing. So back to the drawing board, again and again, until it came together. I got it right in the end, and it took a while, but it was never frustrating. I was able to focus on the logic, the art and the fun.

4 Publishing games is easy and in my case, it was as simple as pressing "export" and uploading it to my web server. But perhaps the most fun element of all this is watching somebody play your game – unprompted – and come at it with fresh eyes. Seeing someone try and jump that tricky platform and fail, but want to try again, is really inspiring. Having tried it for two weeks, I can honestly say my favourite game this year is my own.

2 Choose the best heading for paragraphs 1–4.

Show the world your work   Experiment with simple tools

Use forums to get ideas   Create your characters

Reading tip

In the first paragraph, the writer describes the usual first step when making a computer game. In the second paragraph, he reveals that he did not follow this step. It's important, therefore, to read a whole text, not just to focus on one paragraph, before concluding what the writer is trying to say.

3 Read again and choose the best answer.

1 The author states that exploring ideas is …

   a time consuming.   **b** inspiring.   **c** ineffectual.

2 The author designed his own character for the game because …

   a it was his only option.

   b he wanted to make the game his own.

   c it was easier than using pre-made characters.

3 The author was able to solve the ladder problem by …

   a getting the solution from someone in a forum.

   b drawing it out on paper.

   c persevering and trying different techniques.

4 Read these extracts from the article and choose the best meaning for each.

1 'Only when I'd followed a few tutorials, made a little guy move about and realised "hey, I can do this" was I able to have confidence to dream a little bigger.' (paragraph 1)

   a I used tutorials to find out how to bring my dreams to life.

   b Once I'd seen some tutorials, I felt more ambitious.

2 'While I have some experience as an artist, I still found animating characters surprisingly time consuming until I got into a groove.' (paragraph 2)

   a When I got used to it, I got faster at animating characters.

   b Animating characters was slow because I kept making errors.

3 'But perhaps the most fun element of all this is watching somebody play your game – unprompted – and come at it with fresh eyes.' (paragraph 4)

   a By watching someone play your game, you get new ideas.

   b It's good to see someone new playing the game voluntarily.

Next steps

Read some books or websites about your hobby and note down some specialist vocabulary.

Think about how best to organize this vocabulary so it is easy to learn and retrieve.

19 HUMOUR
Jokes and word play

Getting started

1 Do you enjoy reading joke books and cartoons?
2 Have you ever read any jokes in English?
3 Do you think jokes in other languages can be funny?

A   Cartoons

1 **Write the letters a–e in the correct speech bubbles. Do you find the jokes funny?**

a How long has your house been on the market, Brian?

b Doctor, I'm not a tall well.

c No, I'm a very heavy sleeper.

d Don't worry, you'll pick it up as you go along.

e He wanted 50 quid for the wardrobe, but I managed to knock him down.

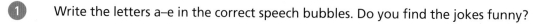

1

COUNCIL LITTER
COLLECTION
DEPOT.

I DON'T KNOW IF
I CAN DO THIS JOB

2

17"

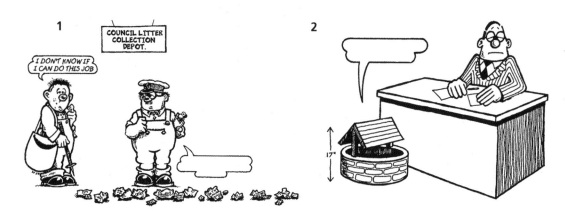

3

DON'T THESE TRACKS
KEEP YOU AWAKE?

4

5

Language note

Many words in English have two or more meanings, and many jokes are based around this. This kind of joke is called a pun.

Why did the cross-eyed teacher get fired?

She couldn't control her pupils.

Pupil / ˈpjuːpəl /

1 a child who is taught by a teacher **2** the black circle in the centre of the eye

B Puns

1 Complete the jokes with a noun to produce a double meaning.

reception	tank	balance	ground

1 There were two fish in a .... One says: 'How do you drive this thing?'.

2 Two television aerials met on a roof, fell in love and got married. The .... was brilliant.

3 I went to a bank and asked the clerk if she would check my ...., so she pushed me over.

4 'This coffee tastes like mud!'. 'Well, it was .... only a few minutes ago!'.

2 Underline the word with a double meaning, and note down the two definitions.

1 What did one ocean say to the other ocean? Nothing, they just waved.

2 I asked the gym instructor 'Can you teach me to do the splits?'. 'I'm not sure. How flexible are you?'. I said, 'I can't make Tuesdays'.

3 A man got hit on the head with a can of cola. Luckily it was a soft drink.

4 I wanted to lose weight so I went to a paint store. I heard I could get thinner there.

3 Which cartoons on pages 88–89 are based on a word's double meaning?

Language note

Homophones sound like other words, but have different spellings and meanings: *where* and *wear*, *poor* and *pour* or *eight* and *ate*. Many English jokes play on the double meaning of a word's sound.

> Why is 6 afraid of 7?
>
> Because 7 8 9. *(Because 7 ate 9)*

In some jokes, two words sound like one other word.

> Two peanuts were walking in a bad part of town. One of them was a salted.
>
> *a salted (peanut) = a peanut with salt*
>
> *assaulted = attacked*

4 In the following jokes, underline the homophone. What word or phrase does the homophone sound like?

1 Two hats were hanging on a hat rack in the hallway. One hat says to the other, 'You stay here, I'll go on ahead.'

2 How do you make antifreeze? Steal her blanket.

3 You jumped off a bridge in Paris? You must be insane!

4 There was a fire at the campsite. The heat was intense.

5 Match the beginnings to the ends of each joke.

1 Yesterday I accidentally swallowed some blue food colouring.

2 After my accident, the doctors had to cut off my left leg and my left arm.

3 I decided to quit my job as a doctor.

4 I've decided to marry a pencil.

a I feel like I've dyed a little inside.

b I can't wait to introduce my parents to my bride 2B.

c I had no patience.

d I'm all right now.

6 Which cartoon on the first page is based on a homophone?

Reading tip

Some jokes utilize the double meanings of idioms and phrasal verbs – the literal meaning and the idiomatic one.

I wondered why the baseball was getting bigger. Then it hit me.

Literal meaning:	*The baseball hit me.*
Idiomatic meaning:	*'It hit me' = I suddenly realized.*

I used to have a fear of hurdles, but I got over it.

Literal meaning:	*I jumped over a hurdle.*
Idiomatic meaning:	*'I got over it' = I overcame my fear.*

---

7 Underline the word or phrase with two meanings.

1 How do you communicate with a fish? Just drop them a line.

2 My friend lost his job at the road department for stealing. I didn't believe it at first, but the other day I went to his house and all the signs were there.

3 Yesterday, I went to an electrical store and I saw a TV on sale for £1, but the volume was stuck on full. I said, 'How can I turn that down?'

4 I couldn't work out how to fasten my seatbelt. Then it clicked.

8 Which cartoons on pages 88–89 use both the literal and idiomatic meaning of a phrasal verb?

Next steps

Read some jokes on the website Pun of the Day – **www.punoftheday.com**. Can you find five puns that make you laugh?

Do an online search for 'funniest jokes'. Which one do you like best? Tell it to your friends!

---

20 INSPIRATIONAL ACCOUNTS
An autobiography

Getting started

1 What kind of books do you most enjoy reading?
2 How do you choose which books to read?
3 What book has inspired you the most?

A   An autobiography

1   Read the summary of Malcolm X's life and complete the notes.

Born Malcolm Little on May 19, 1925, Malcolm X was one of the most articulate and powerful leaders of black America during the 1960s. A street hustler convicted of robbery in 1946, he spent seven years in prison, where he educated himself and became a disciple of Elijah Muhammad, founder of the Nation of Islam. In the days of the civil rights movement, Malcolm X emerged as the leading spokesman for black separatism, a philosophy that urged black Americans to cut political, social, and economic ties with the white community. After a pilgrimage to Mecca, the capital of the Muslim world, in 1964, he became an orthodox Muslim, adopted the Muslim name El Hajj Malik El-Shabazz, and distanced himself from the teachings of the black Muslims.

He was assassinated in 1965. In the following excerpt from his autobiography (1965), coauthored with Alex Haley and published the year of his death, Malcolm X describes his self-education.

Year of birth / year of death: ....

Country: ....

He was famous as: ....

Religion: ....

2   Autobiographies tend to be written by people who have had exceptional lives. They may have overcome a problem, realized a dream or inspired others. Read an excerpt from Malcolm X's autobiography. What problem did he overcome and where was he when he overcame it?

1 It was because of my letters that I happened to stumble upon starting to acquire some kind of a homemade education.

2 I became increasingly frustrated at not being able to express what I wanted to convey in letters that I wrote, especially those to Mr. Elijah Muhammad. In the street, I had been the most articulate hustler out there. I had commanded attention when I said something. But now, trying to write simple English, I not only wasn't articulate, I wasn't even functional. How would I sound writing in slang, the way I would say it, something such as, "Look, daddy, let me pull your coat about a cat, Elijah Muhammad—"

3 It had really begun back in the Charlestown Prison, when Bimbi first made me feel envy of his stock of knowledge. Bimbi had always taken charge of any conversations he was in, and I had tried to emulate him. But every book I picked up had few sentences which didn't contain anywhere from one to nearly all of the words that might as well have been in Chinese. When I just skipped those words, of course, I really ended up with little idea of what the book said. So I had come to the Norfolk Prison Colony still going through only book-reading motions. Pretty soon, I would have quit even these motions, unless I had received the motivation that I did.

4 I saw that the best thing I could do was get hold of a dictionary—to study, to learn some words. I was lucky enough to reason also that I should try to improve my penmanship. It was sad. I couldn't even write in a straight line. It was both ideas together that moved me to request a dictionary along with some tablets and pencils from the Norfolk Prison Colony school.

5 I spent two days just riffling uncertainly through the dictionary's pages. I'd never realized so many words existed! I didn't know which words I needed to learn. Finally, just to start some kind of action, I began copying.

6 In my slow, painstaking, ragged handwriting, I copied into my tablet everything printed on that first page, down to the punctuation marks.

7 I believe it took me a day. Then, aloud, I read back, to myself, everything I'd written on the tablet. Over and over, aloud, to myself, I read my own handwriting.

This text continues on page 94.

8 I woke up the next morning, thinking about those words—immensely proud to realize that not only had I written so much at one time, but I'd written words that I never knew were in the world. Moreover, with a little effort, I also could remember what many of these words meant. I reviewed the words whose meanings I didn't remember. Funny thing, from the dictionary first page right now, that "aardvark" springs to my mind. The dictionary had a picture of it, a long-tailed, long-eared, burrowing African mammal, which lives off termites caught by sticking out its tongue as an anteater does for ants.

9 I was so fascinated that I went on—I copied the dictionary's next page. And the same experience came when I studied that. With every succeeding page, I also learned of people and places and events from history. Actually the dictionary is like a miniature encyclopedia. Finally the dictionary's A section had filled a whole tablet—and I went on into the B's. That was the way I started copying what eventually became the entire dictionary. It went a lot faster after so much practice helped me to pick up handwriting speed. Between what I wrote in my tablet, and writing letters, during the rest of my time in prison I would guess I wrote a million words.

This text continues on page 96.

3 **Before reading further, answer the following questions.**

1 Why did Malcolm want to learn how to read and write?

   a To remember what Elijah Muhammed had taught him.

   b To communicate with Elijah Muhammed in writing.

   c To prove that he was as clever as Bimbi.

2 How did Malcolm know Bimbi?

   a They had both been street hustlers.

   b They had both been in Charlestown Prison.

   c They were in Norfolk Prison Colony together.

3 How did Malcolm learn to read and write?

   a He attended the Norfolk Prison Colony school.

   b He read widely, using a dictionary to look up new words.

   c He taught himself by copying a dictionary.

4 Which sentence is true about Malcolm's study technique?

   a He concentrated on writing words he already understood.

   b He drew pictures to help him remember meanings.

   c He re-examined his work the following day.

5 What did Malcolm discover as he continued his project?

   a People respected the knowledge he acquired.

   b He was able to write faster.

   c He used a wider range of words in conversation.

4 Match each verb to its correct meaning.

1 stumble upon (paragraph 1)   a to do something without interest

2 emulate (paragraph 3)   b remember quickly

3 go through the motions (paragraph 3)   c discover by chance

4 spring to mind (paragraph 8)   d increase or improve

5 pick up (paragraph 9)   e copy someone you admire

5 What do you think of Malcolm's technique for learning to read and write? Think of at least one advantage and one disadvantage of his strategy.

Language note

Biographies and autobiographies are often very emotive as they show the central character's journey through difficult periods. Emotions may be described explicitly, for example by using adjectives, or implicitly, through the character's actions or words.

6 Highlight words in the text on pages 93–94 that show Malcolm X's emotions.

7 Which adjectives best describe the author's feelings at different stages of the story?

1 Malcolm was far more ... as a speaker than as a writer.

   a confident   b frustrated   c inarticulate

2 Malcolm felt ... Bimbi's literacy.

   a respect for   b mistrustful of   c motivated by

3 When Malcolm first picked up a dictionary he felt ... .

   a inspired   b doubtful   c unenthusiastic

4 After copying one page of the dictionary Malcolm felt ... .

   a pleased   b discouraged   c ignorant

8 Which adjective describes Malcolm X's emotion in each of the following paragraphs?

enthused	disheartened	bewildered	resolute

Paragraph 3 ....   Paragraph 6 ....

Paragraph 5 ....   Paragraph 9 ....

B An inspiring account

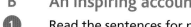 Read the sentences for paragraphs 10–12 below and on the opposite page. Which sentence gives the best overview of each paragraph?

Paragraph 10

a Reading made Malcolm X a better conversationalist and correspondent.

b Reading made Malcolm X neglect his visitors and correspondents.

c Reading broadened Malcolm X's horizons and liberated him.

10 I suppose it was inevitable that as my word-base broadened, I could for the first time pick up a book and read and now begin to understand what the book was saying. Anyone who has read a great deal can imagine the new world that opened. Let me tell you something: from then until I left that prison, in every free moment I had, if I was not reading in the library, I was reading on my bunk. You couldn't have gotten me out of books with a wedge. Between Mr. Muhammad's teachings, my correspondence, my visitors—usually Ella and Reginald—and my reading of books, months passed without my even thinking about being imprisoned. In fact, up to then, I never had been so truly free in my life.

11 The teachings of Mr. Muhammad stressed how history had been "whitened"—when white men had written history books, the black man simply had been left out. I never will forget how shocked I was when I began reading about slavery's total horror. It made such an impact upon me that it later became one of my favorite subjects when I became a minister of Mr. Muhammad's. The world's most monstrous crime, the sin and the blood on the white man's hands, are almost impossible to believe. I read descriptions of atrocities, saw those illustrations of black slave women tied up and flogged with whips; of black mothers watching their babies being dragged off, never to be seen by their mothers again; of dogs after slaves, and of the fugitive slave catchers, evil white men with whips and clubs and chains and guns.

12 I have often reflected upon the new vistas that reading opened to me. I knew right there in prison that reading had changed forever the course of my life. As I see it today, the ability to read awoke inside me some long dormant craving to be mentally alive. I certainly wasn't seeking any degree, the way a college confers a status symbol upon its students. My homemade education gave me, with every additional book that I read, a little bit more sensitivity to the deafness, dumbness, and blindness that was afflicting the black race in America. Not long ago, an English writer telephoned me from London, asking questions. One was, "What's your alma mater?" I told him, "Books." You will never catch me with a free fifteen minutes in which I'm not studying something I feel might be able to help the black man.

Paragraph 11

a   Malcolm X was appalled by the new things he was learning.

b   Malcolm X was horrified by the amount of detail in the books.

c   Malcolm was pleased that he could finally read about his favourite topic.

Paragraph 12

a   Reading gave Malcolm X status.

b   Reading transformed Malcolm X irreversibly.

c   Reading inspired Malcolm X to get a degree.

2   Read the sentences from the autobiography and choose the correct meaning.

1   *You couldn't have gotten me out of books with a wedge.* (paragraph 10)

a   It was impossible to find a book that Malcolm X didn't enjoy.

b   It was impossible to separate Malcolm X from his books.

2   *The teachings of Mr. Muhammad stressed how history had been "whitened".* (paragraph 11)

a   Mr Muhammad taught him that history books never describe terrible things in detail.

b   Mr Muhammad taught him that history books are written from one race's point of view.

3   *As I see it today, the ability to read awoke inside me some long dormant craving to be mentally alive.* (paragraph 12)

a   Reading allowed Malcolm X to use his brain, as, deep-down, he had always wanted to.

b   Until he started reading, Malcolm X had always, deep-down, felt inferior to other people.

3   The extract gives clues as to what happened later in Malcolm X's life. What do you think Malcolm was inspired to do after leaving prison?

4   Autobiographies can be inspiring to the reader. What does Malcolm X's autobiography inspire you to do?

5   What do you know about these inspiring people? Choose two people, then go online and find out about what they did and how they did it.

a   Nelson Mandela

b   Mahatma Gandhi

c   Mother Theresa

d   Martin Luther King Jnr.

e   Lily Ledbetter

f   Rosa Parks

Next steps

Read more about Malcolm X on Wikipedia or elsewhere online.

Read an extract from someone's autobiography. Choose three paragraphs and identify what emotion is primarily described in each.

APPENDIX 1 – Reading skills for the Common European Framework

The Common European Framework (CEF) describes the skills and knowledge that language learners need to communicate effectively. It also measures progress and sets targets at each stage of learning.

Below are the reading skills that B2 and C1 level learners should be aiming to perfect, along with suggestions of how to develop these skills.

1. B2

CEF 'can do' statement: I can read articles and reports concerned with contemporary problems in which writers adopt particular attitudes or viewpoints.

How can I practise this? Read articles from different English language newspapers. Most newspapers have a particular readership; that is, they cater for a particular socio-economic or political group. Find out the readership of the newspaper you are reading, and, as you read, think about how the article caters for this particular group. Consider use of idioms and jokes; length of words, sentences and paragraphs; whether or not specialist vocabulary is used, what emotions, if any, the article seeks to arouse, and think about why the journalist chose to use such literary techniques.

Practice opportunities in this book: Unit 13 News reports

CEF 'can do' statement: I can understand contemporary literary prose.

How can I practise this? Read novels. If you feel uncomfortable about reading a complete book, try a graded reader instead. These are abridged versions of popular novels, making them a more easy-going read. You could also try reading English-language versions of books you have already read and enjoyed in your own language. A further option is to read short stories, which will give you authentic language in more manageable chunks.

Practice opportunities in this book: Unit 20 Inspirational accounts

CEF 'can do' statement: I can adapt my style and speed of reading to different texts and purposes.

Make sure you are familiar with the different reading styles: skimming, where you read a passage quickly to get the general idea of its content; scanning, where you look out for particular information, and reading for detail, where you read every sentence carefully to get its full meaning.

To practise skimming, choose a text and set yourself a time limit of one or two minutes to read the article to the end. Then write a sentence that summarizes the main gist of the article. Re-read the article using the same time limit, and amend your summary sentence if necessary.

To practise scanning, choose a text and, setting yourself a time limit, answer the questions: who, where, what, why, when; that is, who are the people involved in the story, where did the story take place, what happened, why did it happen and when did it happen. Then, without looking at the article, write down three more questions that you expect the article to answer. Set yourself a time limit to find out whether your questions are answered in the text.

To practise reading in detail, read an instruction manual, follow a recipe or find a website that teaches you how to do something. Read every sentence carefully, using a dictionary to make sure you understand each step in the process before moving on.

Practice opportunities in this book: Skimming: Unit 14 Formal discussion; Scanning: Unit 9 Holiday plans; Reading for detail: Unit 18 Interests and hobbies

CEF 'can do' statement: I can use different reference sources selectively.

Familiarize yourself with a variety of dictionaries. Compare your electronic dictionary, if you have one, with online dictionaries and traditional dictionaries. Judge them according to different criteria: ease of use, how clear or comprehensive the definitions are, and what other features are provided, such as example sentences, synonyms, idioms and pronunciation. Get to know other types of reference books too, such as those focusing on idioms, phrasal verbs or subject-specific dictionaries, which are particularly useful for academic study.

CEF 'can do' statement: I have a broad active reading vocabulary, but I may experience some difficulty with low frequency idioms.

The first step in understanding idioms is recognizing them! If you find yourself re-reading a sentence several times, unable to grasp the meaning, or if a familiar word appears in a sentence completely out of context, chances are you are reading an idiom. First, try to identify which words are part of the idiom and which are not. Write out the sentence but omit the idiom – just leave a gap. Then think of other words that could fill the gap and make sense of the sentence. Then look up the meaning of the idiom and see whether you were right.

Practice opportunities in this book: Unit 4 Sharing news

CEF 'can do' statement: I can read correspondence relating to my field of interest and readily grasp the essential meaning.

Register online with a company that you like, such as a retailer, charity, book club or English-language social networking site, e.g. Twitter. A wealth of different styles of correspondence will come your way via email, including offers, updates, details of events and news. Skim each email and take note of what is being said.

Practice opportunities in this book: Unit 1 Invitations

CEF 'can do' statement: I can quickly identify the content and relevance of news items, articles and reports on a wide range of professional topics, deciding whether closer study is worthwhile.

Choose a topic, e.g. a subject that you are studying or something that you're interested in, and identify a number of questions that you'd like to answer.

If you are working online, perform a keyword search to find sources that may answer your question. Skim the titles in the search results and choose three sources to read. Skim these and decide which one contains the most information on your topic. Scan your chosen article and find out if it answers your questions.

If using a library, perform a keyword search on the library catalogue. Alternatively, browse the books on the shelves. Check the contents and index to find out whether the book contains information on your topic. Skim the relevant chapters or pages to find the answers to your questions.

Remember that there are many different sources available. Don't stick with books that are out-dated, over-complicated or simplistic. If you are not getting on with one text, try another.

Practice opportunities in this book: Unit 13 News reports

CEF 'can do' statement: I can obtain information, ideas and opinions from highly specialised sources within my field, and I can understand specialised articles outside my field, provided I can use a dictionary occasionally to confirm my interpretation of terminology.

Read widely on any topic of interest to you: an academic subject, information related to a hobby, or a news item. Each time, read three different types of text. Consider formal texts such as news reports and encyclopaedia entries, as well as informal texts such as blogs, Twitter feeds and forums. Keep a vocabulary book and use a dictionary to define unfamiliar terms. Note down any vocabulary that occurs in at least two texts, as these will most likely be related to the field. As you practise, progress to topics that are outside your immediate field of interest, and reduce your dependence on the dictionary by only looking up the meanings of words you cannot deduce from the context.

Practice opportunities in this book: Unit 15 Opinion pieces

2. C1

CEF 'can do' statement: I can identify finer points of detail including attitudes and implied as well as stated opinions.

Read literature where there is emphasis on character study, such as classic literature and plays. After reading a section, make notes on the personalities of each character in the story, and the various relationships between characters. At first, only note your impressions. Then look for quotations from the text that back up your opinions. Are any of your impressions implied, rather than explicitly stated? How does the writer give you this impression?

CEF 'can do' statement: I can understand long and complex factual and literary texts, appreciating distinctions of style.

Read contrasting texts on the same topic, for example: a modern and a classic novel; prose and poetry; fiction and non-fiction; an encyclopaedia and a blog, or two different genres of fiction. Consider how the two texts differ in terms of the vocabulary and grammatical style used.

Practice opportunities in this book: Unit 17 Creative descriptions: Poetry

APPENDIX 2 – Reading study tips

While you read

Using a dictionary

A dictionary is a vital tool in the language learner's toolbox, but train yourself not to become too dependent on it. When reading an article for the first time, try not to open your dictionary at all. When you finish, summarize the main points of the article. Then go back and reread the article more carefully, looking up unknown words only where necessary. Then look again at your summary to see whether you really needed to use your dictionary to understand the main points of the text.

Keeping a vocabulary notebook

When you have finished reading a text, go back over it and write down any useful new words in a vocabulary notebook. Organize this topic-by-topic or letter-by-letter and try to learn several new words every day. Test yourself by rereading texts that you have read before to see if you can remember the words that you wrote down in your notebook the first time.

Using a pen/pencil

You might find it useful to read texts with a pen or pencil in hand.

- Underline important sentences or phrases while you are reading.
- Write notes in the margin to summarize paragraphs.
- Try using a number of different highlighter pens to colour code different items of new vocabulary.

Remember not to write in borrowed newspapers or books though!

Taking notes

A good way to ensure that you understand what you are reading is to take notes on a text.

- As you read a text or section of text, underline or highlight key sentences or words.
- When you have finished, look back over the highlighted sentences or words and extract the main ideas – you can leave out details, examples and illustrations.
- Don't copy sections of text – write notes using your own words.
- Don't write full sentences, just the important words that carry the meaning.
- Use a form of shorthand that you understand.
- Finally, reread the text and compare it to your notes to make sure that you have included all the main points.

Writing a summary

To summarize a text, you must condense the information in a text into a shortened form (usually between 15 and 20 percent of the original).

- First, take notes on the main ideas of the text (see *Taking notes* above).
- Then, turn the notes into full sentences.
- Finally, compare the text with your summary to ensure that you have included all the main points.

Within the text

Contents list

A contents list is a good place to start when trying to find a particular section of a book. You do not have to read every word in the contents – ignore words at the beginning such as 'introduction' or 'how to use this book' and the end, such as 'appendix', 'glossary' or 'index'. Instead, focus on the chapter headings to give you an idea of how the book is divided up and keep your eyes peeled for key words that might be related to the section you are looking for.

Topic sentences

The first sentence of each paragraph (the topic sentence) often summarizes what the whole paragraph is about. This is helpful when you are skim reading for gist because you can work out what an article or blog is about by simply reading the topic sentences.

Signposting language

Watch out for words and phrases that a writer uses to help you find your way around the text. For example, they may order a list of items with 'firstly', 'secondly', 'thirdly' and 'finally'.

Illustrations and pictures

Illustrations such as graphs or maps are useful in helping you to understand the text. If you are just skimming for gist, make sure you cast your eye over any pictures and their captions that might help you to understand the text more quickly.

Using the Internet

Search engines

There are an estimated 9.7 billion webpages available to read on the Internet and there are more pages in English than in any other language. The quantity of information can sometimes be overwhelming, so use search engines to help you to find the correct page. When you get to the website that you are looking for, check to see if there is a search field for that particular website. If not, scan over the screen for key words that might help you.

Search by reading level

Google has a very helpful search tool, whereby you can sort webpages by reading level. To do this, search for your topic as usual, then on the left hand side of the screen, click on, 'More search tools', and from this menu, click on, 'Reading level'. Then click on your reading level ('Basic', 'Intermediate' or 'Advanced') and it will list just these pages for you.

APPENDIX 3 – Improving your reading speed

Improving your reading speed is a good challenge to set yourself, but remember that speed is not the most important thing when it comes to reading. There is no point in being able to read quickly if you don't understand what you have read. However, there are techniques that you can practise which will help you to read more quickly without compromising on understanding. The more you practise, the faster you will read.

Choosing the right texts

It has been shown that people read more quickly when they enjoy what they are reading, so choose what you read very carefully. Make sure that:

- you are interested in what you're reading. Try reading a wide variety of different texts to find subjects you like. If you are interested in the story, then you are more likely to have the motivation to read (quickly) to the end.
- it is at an appropriate language level for you. If it's too easy, you will get bored and if it's too difficult, you will get lost. When reading for pleasure, you may prefer to choose texts that are a bit easier than those in your textbooks.

Skim read first

A good way to improve how fast you read is to skim through a text first to work out the gist of what is being said. Pay attention to any headings or charts that might help you. Then when you read the text in detail, you will understand it more quickly than if you were looking at it for the first time, and read faster as a result. Obviously this is not appropriate for longer texts, for example novels, but can be used with shorter texts, for example websites or newspaper articles.

Reading chunks of text

Reading a text is like doing a jigsaw – you must piece together the individual words in order to understand the whole. A jigsaw with lots of small pieces takes much longer to put together than one with just a few large pieces. So, if you can train yourself to read chunks of text at a time (made up of three to five words) rather than reading each word individually, then it won't take you so long to piece together the meaning. For example, when reading, you might group together the following chunks of this sentence from Unit 14.

'For the first time / researchers claim to have shown that / the increase in plant cover / is due to / this CO_2 fertilisation effect / rather than any other causes.'

There are no hard and fast rules for grouping words into chunks and you should find a way that works for you, but you could consider grouping:

- words that form an adverbial phrase, such as 'for the first time' and 'is due to'; a noun phrase, such as 'increase in plant cover'; or a verb phrase such as 'claim to have shown'.
- parts of speech that go together; for example, articles with nouns (*the* increase in plant cover / *this* CO_2 fertilisation effect) and subjects with verbs (*Researchers* claim to have shown) and conjunctions (*Researchers* claim to have shown *that*).

Use a pointer

A good way of improving your reading speed is to run your finger or a pen beneath each line of a book as you read. Make sure you keep moving your finger or pen at a regular speed and do not stop to look up unknown words. Do not be tempted to go back and reread sentences because this will slow you down. If necessary, come back and review sentences that you have missed at the end if they have stopped you from understanding the overall meaning of the text. If you find this difficult, use a piece of paper or a ruler to cover up the line you have just read to prevent you from going backwards.

Read in your head

Don't read aloud and don't even move your lips silently when you're reading because this will prevent you from reading faster than you can speak, even though your brain is capable of taking in information much more quickly than this. However, this is not to say that you should never read aloud — it's a great way to practise your pronunciation and build your confidence. Just remember that it may slow you down. So practise both methods – read in your head when trying to improve your reading speed and read aloud to help your pronunciation.

Focus on the most important words

When reading, some words are more important than others. Concentrate on the words that carry the meaning, for example, the nouns, verbs and adjectives. Pay less attention to the words that hold the sentence together, for example, conjunctions, prepositions or articles. For instance, in this sentence you might focus on the words in bold and let your eyes skim over the other words:

'**Critics**, however, will **argue** that the **noises** will **ruin** the **simple pleasure** of having the **imagination stimulated** by **reading**.'

Time yourself and track your progress

A native speaker of English will read an average of 300 words per minute. If you want to find out how many words you read per minute and, more importantly, track your progress at improving your reading speed, then carry out the following. Choose a text from this book to read and set a stopwatch to time you two minutes. When you have finished, summarize the passage to make sure that you have understood it. Then count the number of words that you have read and divide it by two to work out how many words you read per minute. Test yourself every few weeks to see if you are getting faster. There are also numerous websites which you can use to test your reading speed.

Bear in mind that we read different types of text at different speeds, and that when we are reading for detail and understanding we will read much more slowly than when we read for pleasure.

Abbreviations used in this book

24/7	24 hours a day, 7 days a week
ad	advertisement
asap	as soon as possible
BNIB	brand new in box
BTW	by the way
est.	established
eves	evenings
EXPWY	expressway
FAQ	frequently asked question
GDP	Gross Domestic Product
hrs	hours
HWY	highway
i.e.	in other words
IMHO	In my humble opinion
IOU	I owe you
LN	lane (street name)
mph	miles per hour
no.	number
OAP	old age pensioner
ONO	or nearest offer
PL	Place (for street names)
RRP	Recommended Retail Price
RSVP	Please reply (Repondez s'il vous plait)
ST	street
VGC	very good condition

Other common abbreviations

FYI	For your information
NB	Please note
PS	Post script (at the end of a letter)
vs	versus

Abbreviations used in text messages and instant messaging

B4	Before
BRB	Be right back
CU	See you
Gr8	Great
IDK	I don't know
L8R	later
LOL	Laughing out loud
ROFL	Rolling on the floor laughing
THX	thanks
TTFN	Ta-ta (Goodbye) for now

Some of the most interesting idioms and phrasal verbs from each unit are defined here in this mini-dictionary. Most of the definitions are taken from the *Collins COBUILD Phrasal Verbs Dictionary* and the *Collins COBUILD Idioms Dictionary*. All definitions focus specifically on the meanings of the words and phrases in the contexts in which they appear in this book.

Unit 1

Idioms

not miss something for the world If you say that you would **not miss something for the world**, you mean that it is important to you and you would never want to miss it. • *I love this festival. I wouldn't miss it for the world.*

Phrasal Verbs

make it If you cannot **make it**, you are unable to attend an event that you have been invited to. • *He wasn't able to make it to our party.*

fly by If time **flies by** it seems to pass very quickly. • *Time really does fly by when you're having a good time.*

pop in If you **pop in**, you go to a friend's house or a shop for a short time. • *They sometimes pop in for a coffee and a chat.*

reach out If you **reach out** to people, you give them help, advice, or comfort. • *He has a wonderful ability to reach out to people.*

turn down If you **turn** something or someone **down**, you refuse a request or offer. • *I turned down an invitation for Saturday.*

Unit 2

Phrasal Verbs

make up If you **make up** time, you work extra hours because you have previously taken time off work. • *Can I leave early today? I'll work on Saturday to make it up.*

pick up If you **pick** something **up**, you buy it. • *If you're after a camera, you can probably pick one up cheaply here.*

Unit 3

Idioms

get on someone's nerves [INFORMAL] If someone or something **gets on** your **nerves**, they irritate you.• *Camilla likes him but he gets on my nerves.*

go out of your way If you **go out of your way** to do something, you make an extra effort to do it. • *It seemed as if Richard had gone out of his way to be offensive.*

grin and bear it If you **grin and bear it**, you accept or tolerate something bad, such as a problem or a pain, because you believe you cannot change it. • *In the past, a royal trapped in a loveless marriage would have been obliged to grin and bear it.*

look as if (someone / something) have been dragged through a hedge backwards If you say that someone looks as if they have been **dragged through a hedge backwards**, you mean that their hair or clothes look very untidy.• *I looked as if I had been dragged through a hedge backwards when I woke up this morning.*

make a big deal (out) of something If you **make a big deal out of** something, you make a fuss about it or treat it as if were very important. [INFORMAL] • *She always made a big deal out of the way people spelled her name.*

make fun of someone If you **make fun of** someone, you laugh at them, tease them, or make jokes about them in a way that causes them to seem ridiculous. • *They make fun of me at school.*

take something to heart If you **take** someone's advice or criticism **to heart**, you pay a lot of attention to it, and are greatly influenced or upset by it. • *You know he says nasty things when he's angry. Don't take it to heart, Polly.*

Phrasal Verbs

distance yourself If you **distance yourself from** a person or thing, you show that you are not involved with them, especially to avoid trouble or blame. • *Guillotin tried to distance himself from the debate.*

even out If people **even out**, they become more equal or similar and the differences between them become less noticeable. • *Later in life, perhaps everyone evens out, but in the first years, those born prematurely seem to have more struggles.*

get away with If you **get away with** something that you should not have done, you are not criticized or punished for doing it. • *You mustn't let him get away with it when he's rude to you like that.*

get to If an experience **gets to** you, it upsets or annoys you. [INFORMAL] • She can be quite rude sometimes but don't let it get to you.

hang out with If you **hang out with** someone, you spend time with that person in a social situation. hang out with someone • He spends a lot of time hanging out with friends.

mess with If you **mess with** someone, you make jokes about them or do things in order to annoy or upset them. [INFORMAL] • I thought Johnny was just making up the story to mess with me.

put someone down If you **put someone down**, you criticize them and make them feel stupid. • Another thing that upsets me is the way Alex tries to put me down in public.

shoot up If someone **shoots up**, they grow taller very quickly. • Your children have really shot up since the last time I saw them.

take up If you **take up** an activity or a job, you start doing it. • I thought I'd take up fishing.

turn to If you **turn to** someone, you ask them for help or advice. • I have no other friend to turn to.

work out If you **work out**, you do physical exercises in order to make your body healthy and • She worked out in a ballet class three hours a week.

Unit 4

Idioms

be in their element If you are **in** your **element**, you are doing something that you enjoy and do well. • My stepmother was in her element, organizing everything.

bundle of joy [INFORMAL] **A bundle of joy** is a baby, especially one that has just been born. • Our family are overjoyed at the early arrival of our little bundle of joy.

eat for two If a woman is **eating for two**, she is eating more than usual because she is pregnant. • Victoria made the classic mistake of eating for two when she was pregnant.

fly the nest When children **fly the nest** or **leave the nest**, they leave their parents' home to live on their own. • When their children had flown the nest, he and his wife moved to a cottage in Dorset.

go it alone If you **go it alone**, you start your own business after previously working for an employer. • The decision to quit my well-paid job with an agency to go it alone had not been an easy one.

have a lot on your plate If you **have enough on** your **plate** or **have a lot on** your **plate**, you have a lot of work to do or a lot of things to deal with. • I'm sorry to bother you with it, Mark, but John's got enough on his plate.

have had a good innings [BRITISH, OLD-FASHIONED] When someone has just died or is about to die, if you say that they **have had a good innings**, you mean that they have lived for a long time and have had a good life. • Lord knows, I've had a good innings and I'm in pain, Hannah. I want to go.

in good hands If someone or something is **in good hands**, they are being looked after by someone who will make sure they are not harmed or damaged. • Although I knew the children would be in good hands, I still felt anxious.

make the best of something If you **make the best of** something, you deal with a bad or difficult situation as well as you can. • I had made the decision to accept the challenge and make the best of it.

over the moon [BRITISH, INFORMAL] If you are **over the moon** about something that has happened, you are very happy about it. • 'Caroline must be pleased about her new job.' – 'She's over the moon.'

pass with flying colours If you achieve something, such as passing an examination, **with flying colours**, you achieve it easily and are very successful. • She passed the entrance exam with flying colours.

pop the question [INFORMAL] If you **pop the question**, you ask someone to marry you. • Stuart got serious quickly and popped the question six months later.

pull an all-nighter If you **pull an all-nighter**, you study or work all night. • Students were pulling all-nighters to prepare for the exam.

put a word in If you **put a word in**, you tell someone about the good qualities that a particular person has in order to try to help that person. • I got the job mainly because my aunt knew the manager and she put a word in for me.

takes its toll If a problem or a difficult situation **takes its toll**, it causes unpleasant effects. • The bad weather was soon taking its toll on most of the crew members.

take someone for a spin If you **take** someone **for a spin**, you take them for a short journey in your car for pleasure. • He took her for a spin in his sports car.

the big day The big day is that day that someone is getting married. [INFORMAL] • So, when's the big day?

tick all the boxes If someone or something **ticks all the boxes**, they have all the qualities that you want. • If I were looking for my ideal man, Jamie would tick all the boxes.

tie the knot When two people **tie the knot**, they get married. • It was ten years before they actually tied the knot.

time on your hands If you have **time on** your **hands**, you have a lot of free time and you do not know what to do with it. • Jimmy had too much time on his hands and that caused him to get into trouble.

up to your ears If you are **up to your ears** in work or in an unpleasant situation, you are very busy with it or are deeply involved in it. • *I can't come out this evening – I'm up to my ears in reports.*

Phrasal Verbs

bow out of If you **bow out of something**, you stop doing something or taking part in something, often in order to allow someone else to take your place. • *I hear Annie has bowed out of the project.*

catch up If you **catch up**, you talk to a friend that you have not seen for a while, finding out what has happened in his or her life since you last met. • *She plans to return to Dublin to catch up with the relatives she hasn't seen since she married.*

ferry around If you **ferry** someone **around**, you take them by car to several places. • *Now she keeps asking me to ferry her children around.*

fly by *See Unit 1.*

get down If something **gets** you **down**, it makes you unhappy. • *I work all the time and it's really getting me down.*

hang on to If you **hang on to** something, you keep it although it may not be useful or valuable. • *Shall I throw these old magazines out, or do you want to hang onto them?*

keep at If you **keep at it**, or **keep** someone **at it**, you continue, or make them continue, doing something, even if it is difficult or unpleasant. • *It is hard, but you've just got to keep at it.*

pan out If something **pans out**, it develops in a successful way. • *I'll look for a new job if my current one doesn't pan out.*

pass away You can say that someone **passes away** to mean that they die, especially if you want to avoid saying the word 'die'. • *We received his letter shortly before he passed away.*

sign off If you **sign off**, you write or say that you are about to finish a message or broadcast. • *It's time for me to go so I'll sign off now. With love from Dad.*

snap up If you **snap** something **up**, you take advantage of an opportunity as quickly as possible. • *I would have expected him to snap up a chance like this.*

work out If a situation **works out** in a particular way, it happens or progresses in that way. • *I asked him how he was, and how his job was working out.*

Unit 5

Phrasal Verbs

call-out/call out A **call-out** or **call-out charge** is an amount of money that you must pay for someone to come to your house in order to repair something. • *I couldn't afford the call-out charge for the emergency electrician.*

check out If you **check out** a person, place or a thing, you look at them or find out more about them, in order to see whether you like them. [INFORMAL] • *We could check out the new club on Green Street.*

sign up If you **sign up**, you agree to do or take part in something. • *Anyone who signs up for this challenge knows it's not going to be easy.*

take out If you **take out** something such as a licence, an insurance policy, or a bank loan, you arrange to get it. • *I want to take out a mortgage.*

Unit 6

Idioms

a nice touch A **nice touch** is a detail which has been added to something and improves it. • *He left some chocolates on the kitchen table as a welcome, which was a nice touch.*

get to grips with If you **get to grips with** something, you start to deal with it successfully. • *I was longing to get to grips with the new computer game I had bought.*

wear and tear Wear and tear is the damage that happens to something as a result of it being used in a normal way. • *The table in a busy family kitchen is likely to come in for a considerable amount of wear and tear.*

Phrasal Verbs

come across If you **come across** someone or something, you find or meet them by chance. • *He was cleaning out his attic one morning when he came across an old brass lamp.*

could do with If something or someone **could do with** something, they need it. • *You look as though you could do with a hot drink.*

pick up If a piece of equipment such as a radio or microphone **picks up** a signal or sound, it receives or discovers it. • *These bugging devices were capable of picking up both telephone and room conversations.*

keep up with To **keep up with** someone or something means to move or do something at the same speed as them. • *I struggled to keep up with him.*

throw in If you **throw in** an extra item when you are selling something or arranging something, you add or include it to make a deal more attractive to someone. • *She bought the dress after I threw in a matching scarf.*

Unit 7

Phrasal verbs

carry around If you **carry** something **around**, you have it with you, usually in a bag or in your pocket. • *The books were so big that I couldn't carry them around all day.*

Unit 8

Phrasal verbs

breathe in When you **breathe in**, you take air into your lungs through your nose or mouth. • *Breathe in slowly.*

enter into If you **enter into** an agreement or arrangement, you formally agree to it. • *They were asked to enter into a joint project with the company.*

feel like If you **feel like** doing something, you want to do it. • *I just didn't feel like going to work that day.*

give off When objects or processes **give off** heat, light, smoke, or sound, they release it into the air. • *I remember the tremendous heat given off by the fire.*

make up If people or things **make up** something, they form it. • *Women now make up two-fifths of the work force.*

Unit 9

Idioms

have something in spades If you have something **in spades**, you have a lot of it. • *The job required determination and ambition – and she had both qualities in spades.*

Unit 11

Idioms

Phrasal Verbs

take in If you **take** something **in**, you pay attention to it so that you understand, remember, or experience it fully. • *It was all too much to take in.*

tucked away If something or someone **is tucked away**, they are in a quiet place where very few people go. • *The restaurant is tucked away behind the cathedral.*

Unit 12

Idioms

give something a go If you **give** something **a go**, you try to do it. • *We decided to give it a go.*

have time to kill If you **have time to kill**, you have some free time while you are waiting for something else. • *We had four hours to kill before catching the flight.*

(not) catch somebody doing something If you say that you would not **catch** someone **doing** something, you mean that they would never do it. • *You wouldn't catch me wearing a bikini.*

off the beaten track [BRITISH] If a place is **off the beaten track**, it is far away from places where most people live or go. • *The house is sufficiently off the beaten track to deter all but a few tourists.*

the heavens open [BRITISH] If **the heavens open**, it begins to rain very heavily. • *Ten minutes before the start, the sky darkened and the heavens opened.*

Phrasal Verbs

blurt out If you **blurt out** something, you say it suddenly, without thinking about it. • *I hadn't intended to blurt it out like that.*

chicken out [INFORMAL] If you **chicken out**, you decide not to do something because you are afraid. • *I thought of replying but chickened out.*

end up If you **end up in** a particular place or situation, you are in that place or situation after a series of events, even though you did not originally intend to be. • *Two of my friends ended up in prison for armed robbery.*

pick up When you **pick up** someone or something that is waiting to be collected, you go to the place where they are and take them away, often in a car. • *She was going to her parents' house to pick up some clean clothes.*

Unit 13

Phrasal Verbs

bear down on If something large **bears down on** someone or something, it moves quickly towards them in a threatening way. • *We struggled to turn the boat as the wave bore down on us.*

come to If someone **comes to**, they become conscious again after being unconscious. • *That's about all I remember, until I came to in a lifeboat.*

die down If something **dies down** it becomes quieter or weaker or disappears. • *The wind has died down now.*

knock down To **knock** something or someone **down** means to hit them and make them fall to the ground. • *A stolen car went through two fences and knocked down a lamppost.*

tear off To **tear** something **off** means to remove it roughly and violently. • *The storm tore the roof off a hospital and damaged several houses.*

touch down When a severe weather condition such as a storm, tornado, or lightning **touches down**, it hits a place. • *The hurricane is expected to touch down this evening.*

Idioms

lay waste to something If something **lays waste to** something, it completely destroys it. • *The disease itself spread like wildfire, laying waste to whole communities in a matter of days.*

Unit 14

Phrasal Verbs

damp down To **damp down** a particular activity or process is to reduce it. • *The drug damps down the body's immune response.*

home in on If you **home in on** a subject, you pay more attention to it. • *She quickly homed in on the things that worried me most.*

pin down If you try to **pin down** something, you try to say exactly what it is or what it is like. • *Police have managed to pin down when and where he was last seen.*

tear off If you **tear** something **off** or **tear** it **off** something, you remove it from the thing it is attached to by pulling it violently. • *She tore off a leaf and looked at it.*

Unit 15

Idioms

all the trimmings If you say that something has **all the trimmings**, you mean that it has many extra things added to it to make it more special. • *She was going to have a big white wedding with all the trimmings.*

take something lying down If something bad is happening and you say that you will not **take** it **lying down**, you mean that you will complain about it or fight against it. • *It is clear that he means to push everyone out who does not agree with him, and I for one am not going to take it lying down.*

Phrasal verbs

bring something in Someone or something that **brings in** money makes or earns it. • *Tourism is a big industry, bringing in £7 billion a year.*

bring up If you **bring up** a particular subject, you start talking about it. • *I am sorry to bring up the subject of politics yet again.*

go through If you **go through** an event or period of time, especially an unpleasant one, you experience it. • *She went through hell trying to get her son back.*

knock down To **knock down** a building or part of a building means to destroy it, often deliberately.

• *I'd knock the wall down between the front room and dining room.*

lift out of To **lift** a person, organization, or country **out of** a bad situation is to improve the situation they are in. • *The economic measures are intended to lift the country out of recession.*

swallow up If something is **swallowed up** by something else, or if the other thing swallows it up, it becomes part of it and no longer has a separate identity. • *The old centre of the village was being swallowed up by new housing estates.*

Unit 16

Phrasal Verbs

go through If you **go through** an experience or a period of time, especially an unpleasant or difficult one, you experience it. • *South Africa was going through a period of irreversible change.*

knock down To **knock** something or someone **down** means to hit them and make them fall to the ground. • *A stolen car went through two fences and knocked down a lamppost.*

lift out of To **lift** someone **out of** a bad situation means to get them out of that situation. • *The government believes that these measures will lift 700,000 children out of poverty.*

swallow up If something **is swallowed up** by something else, or if the other thing swallows it up, it becomes part of it and no longer has a separate identity. • *The old centre of the village was being swallowed up by new housing estates.*

Unit 18

Phrasal verbs

come at If you **come at** a situation or problem in a particular way, you think about it or deal with it in that

way. • *I tried to come at it from a child's perspective.*

come together If something **comes together**, it starts to be good or effective because its different parts are combining well. • *The team is starting to come together now after a series of problems.*

fire up If you **fire** someone **up**, you make them feel very enthusiastic or angry about something. • *I knew that Sam was trying to fire Costantino up. He kept saying 'You beat him, you beat him'.*

take down If you **take** someone **down**, you defeat or kill them, or have them punished. • *He threatened to take them all down with him if he was caught.*

Idioms

back to the drawing board If you have to go **back to the drawing board**, something which you have done has not been successful and you will have to try another idea. • *His government should go back to the drawing board to rethink their programme in time to return it to the Parliament by September.*

in a groove If someone, especially a sports person or team is **in the groove**, they are performing well. • *Nick is in the groove, as he showed with seven goals last weekend.*

Unit 19

Idioms

all the signs were there If you say that **all the signs were there**, you mean that there was a lot of evidence of something which you did not notice or recognize at the time. • *I felt guilty because all the signs were there and I'd done nothing to help him.*

drop someone a line If you **drop** someone **a line**, you write to them. • *Drop me a line and let me know how you're getting on.*

it clicked If you say **it clicked**, you mean that you suddenly understood or realized something. • *I couldn't think who he was, and then it clicked.*

Phrasal Verbs

knock down If you **knock** someone **down**, you persuade them to reduce the price of something. • *I bought a T-shirt from a street vendor, knocking him down from $10.50 to $8.50.*

pick up If you **pick up** a skill, habit, or attitude, you learn it or start having it after watching and listening to other people. • *I chew gum but I don't want my children to pick up the habit.*

turn down If you **turn** something **down**, you adjust the controls of a device so that it produces less sound or heat. • *Turn the sound down.*

Unit 20

Idioms

cut ties If you **cut ties** with a person or organization, you decide to stop having any relationship or connection with them. • *The singer has cut ties with his recording company.*

get hold of If you **get hold of** something that you need or want, you get it. • *I managed to get hold of a copy.*

take charge If you **take charge** of something, you take control of it and can influence what happens. • *You need the confidence to take charge of your own life.*

Phrasal Verbs

stumble upon If you **stumble upon** something, you find it or discover it unexpectedly. • *I recently stumbled upon a delightful Turkish restaurant.*

ANSWER KEY

Unit 1 Invitations

A Social invitations

1

1 wedding, Westlake Registry Office, Friday 4th June at Twelve o'clock

2 leaving party, meeting room 4, Friday at 5 p.m.

2

1 invitation 1

2 invitation 2

3 invitation 2

4 invitation 1

3

a … request the honour of your presence on …

b Please let me know if you can come.

c I regret that I will not be able to attend.

d Thanks for the invite!

e I wouldn't miss it for the world.

f a prior engagement

4

1 reception

2 do, something on

3 Would love to come

4 It is with deepest regret that, decline

B An invitation to a charity event

1

informal

2

1 2nd anniversary

2 Saturday 12th November

3 Valmont Club

4 9 p.m.

5 £25

6 Smart casual

3

1 charity

2 trauma recovery centre

3 venue, refreshments

4 leaving a donation, get involved as a volunteer

5 book in advance

6 £35 (£25 ticket cost plus £10 entry)

7 complementary soft drink

8 20% discount

9 'like'

10 IBP10, 70070

4

1	e	3	d	5	b
2	f	4	c	6	a

Unit 2 Requests at work

A Everyday requests

1

1 The company wants to be paid.

2 Rachel wants Helen to buy stamps.

3 H. Hodge wants Helen's company to give them an estimate for an alarm system.

4 Jenny wants permission to leave early on Thursday.

2

1 a   2 a   3 b   4 b

3

1 buy stamps this morning

2 speak to Jenny re: leaving early the end of the day

3 pay outstanding balance 23rd July

4 complete bid for alarm system 1st August

4

1 outstanding balance   5 estimate

2 invoice   6 bid

3 interest   7 contract

4 petty cash   8 ample

5

1 Formal requests: Please forward us ... (text 1); I am writing to request ... (text 3); Please submit ... (text 3); Would it be possible for me to ... (text 4); I'd appreciate it if you could (text 4)

2 Informal requests; Please can you ... (text 2); Don't forget to ... (text 2)

3 Those from strangers

4 Those from your employees

5 Yes

B Formal requests

1

1 b   3 c   5 c   7 d

2 a   4 a   6 b   8 a

Unit 3   Online forums

A Asking for advice

1

1 b   2 c   3 c

2

1 She is tall and curvy, overweight, with curly hair. She lacks confidence and is self-conscious. She seems to be dependent on her circle of friends and is nervous about meeting people.

2 They tease her about her body and hair, and the fact that she is trying to lose weight.

3 Misty believes that the teasing is only in fun, but it annoys her as it makes her self-conscious.

B Giving advice

1

1 d   3 e   5 a

2 c   4 f   6 b

2

1 Hannah999 4   4 Kitty14 and SuperGirl

2 Thomas_B   5 SportFan

3 Sergio_82   6 Matt_W

3

1 Kitty 14, Hannah999 and SuperGirl seem most sympathetic.

Suggested answers:

'You deserve to be treated better', 'I know how you feel', 'hun', 'I understand why …'

2 Suggested answer:

Sergio_82. Short answer, short sentences and hasn't taken note of Misty's comment that she doesn't want to find new friends.

3 answers will vary.

4

1 I were you I'd   3 suggest

2 advise you   4 be time to

5

1 b   2 b   3 a

6

1 turn to

2 going out of your way

3 take it to heart

4 make a big deal out of

5 distance yourself from

6 grin and bear it

Unit 4   Sharing news

A   Instant messages

1

1 h	3 d	5 b	7 g
2 a	4 f	6 e	8 c

2

a 1	c 2	e 3	g 4
b 7	d 5	f 8	h 6

3

1	pop the question	5 nest
2	eating for two	6 knot
3	flying colours	7 bundle
4	good innings	8 ferry

Suggested order: 1 pass with flying colours,
2 fly the nest, 3 pop the question, 4 tie the knot,
5 eat for two, 6 have a bundle of joy,
7 ferry someone around, 8 have a good innings

4

1 popped a question → popped the question
2 eating with two → eating for two
3 with a flying colour → with flying colours
4 joy bundle → bundle of joy

5

1 go it alone
2 worked / working out
3 flown the nest
4 tying the knot
5 popped the question
6 bundle of joy
7 eating for two
8 ferry them around

B   Personal letters

1

1 Hannah	3 Simon	5 Kirstin
2 Duncan	4 Rebecca	

2

1 birth	4 a house move	
2 a new job	5 marriage	
3 illness		

3

1 No information	4 No information	
2 T	5 T	
3 F	6 F	

4

1 b	3 a	5 b
2 a	4 a	6 b

5

1 flown by	4 snapped up	
2 bow out	5 pans out	
3 keep at it	6 pop in	

6

1 b	3 a	5 b	7 b
2 b	4 b	6 b	8 a

7

We did manage to get all the photos taken
outdoors (contrast); It does give me a welcome
break from the library (contrast); He does find
driving a lot more stressful than he used to
(contrast); She always did love being in the
countryside (a strong like)

Unit 5   Adverts

A   Classified ads

1

a	driving school	c tuition
b	computer repairs	d health club

2

1 New You	4 Advance Now	
2 The Right Place	5 The Right Place	
3 Education Solutions	6 The Right Place	

3

1	F	5	No information
2	No information	6	F
3	T	7	T
4	No information		

4

1	affordable	5	trial
2	Refer	6	guaranteed
3	obligation	7	bookings
4	call-out	8	apply

B   Special offers

1

1	Silver Fitness	3	Manager's Offer
2	Social You	4	Buddy Pass

2

1	no	4	yes
2	yes	5	no
3	no	6	yes

Unit 6   Online shopping

A   Classified ads

1

1	b	2	a	3	d	4	c

2

1   Cambridge Dacmagic
2   Sony Camera, Apple iPhone
3   Wharfedale Hi-Fi, Cambridge Dacmagic, JVC Camcorder
4   Apple iPad, JVC Camcorder, Sony Camera

3

1	no	2	yes	3	yes	4	no

4

1	crack	5	could do with
2	scratches	6	upgrade
3	wear and tear	7	throw in
4	immaculate	8	warranty

5

1	as new	5	working order
2	open	6	upgraded
3	bargain	7	wear and tear
4	BNIB		

B   Product reviews

1

3

2

1	F	5	T
2	T	6	F
3	No information	7	F
4	No information	8	T

3

Paragraph 2: positive – that's no bad thing, a sophisticated air
Paragraph 6: positive – if you're looking for gaping holes … you're hard-pressed to find them.
Paragraph 7: positive – … the clarity and insight on offer is a match for …
Paragraph 8: positive – … with great aplomb
Paragraph 10: negative – … the Denon holds back
Paragraph 11: negative – … the player struggles to keep you entertained long-term, … this niggle is enough to hold the Denon to a four-star rating

Unit 7   Detailed information

A Operating instructions

1

a

2

1 Before	4 as	7 hence
2 by	5 Once	8 even if
3 If	6 otherwise	

3

Suggested answers:
1 cool food evenly and rapidly
2 hear no liquid moving inside
3 than 1.5 quarts of ingredients
4 an airtight container
5 consistency and flavour

4

1 D	3 –	5 F	7 E
2 C	4 A	6 B	

5

1 consistency		5 substitute
2 thickens		6 tart
3 yield		7 dissolves
4 proportion(s)		8 airtight

6

the kettle and kitchen scales

B Procedures

1

1 no		5 yes
2 yes		6 no
3 yes		7 no
4 not given		

Unit 8   Health and safety

A Warnings

1

1 paint	2 pills	3 washing-up liquid

2

	Product 1	Product 2	Product 3
Store away from children.	✓	✓	✓
Wash if it gets on the skin.	✓		
Go to the doctor if swallowed.	✓		✓

3

1 T	4 T
2 No information	5 F
3 F – Pregnant women should not use product 2	6 T

4

1 ingest	4 prolonged
2 flammable	5 ventilation
3 dose	6 rinse

B Public health warning

1

1 arsenic, benzene, formaldehyde, ammonia
2 lung cancer, heart disease, stroke, asthma

2

| 1 | b | 3 | c | 5 | a | 7 | b |
| 2 | a | 4 | b | 6 | c |

C Written warnings

1

1 gas company   3 employer
2 landlord

2

1 a Not giving gas company access to read the meter
  b call the gas company within ten days to arrange a date for meter reading

c gas will be disconnected and Mark will incur a reconnection charge

2 a Smoking is not permitted in Mark's apartment building.
  b He must not smoke inside, and he must not allow his guests to smoke inside either.
  c His lease will be terminated (i.e. he will be thrown out of his apartment).

3 a Insubordination – bad behaviour at work.
  b He must improve his behaviour.
  c 'Further disciplinary action' and he could lose his job.

3

1 b   2 a   3 e   4 c   5 f   6 d

4

1 unless   3 Provided (that)
2 Failure to   4 Should

Unit 9   Holiday plans

A Travel itineraries

1

Length of tour: 7 days
Countries visited: Brazil, Argentina
Cost: not given
Maximum number of tourists: 16

2

☑ guided tour of Buenos Aires
☐ tango Show
☐ football match
☑ excursion to Iguazú Falls
☐ boat trip below Iguazú Falls
☑ cable car trip up Sugar Loaf Mountain

3

1 not answered   4 Argentinian
2 not answered   5 yes
3 two   6 breakfast only

B A trip dossier

1

Statements 1, 3 and 5 are not accurate.
1 F – they carry a surcharge
3 F – hotels might change
5 F – a budget of around $40 a day should cover the cost of meals

2

A budget of around US$40 per day should cover the cost of meals …

You should not rely exclusively on a card…

We recommend that additionally you take a reasonable quantity …

For day-to-day wear you should take loose-fitting, breathable clothes.

3

You should take a light fleece for cool nights…
1 alone
2 to have as an attribute or result

3 to be sufficient to meet an expense
4 occasional or incidental

5 (of an action or procedure) prevented from occurring

Unit 10 Updates

A Traffic information

1

1 Breaking News   2 Traffic Alerts
3 Motorway Traffic Flow   4 Disruptions Search

2

1 c   2 a   3 d   4 e   5 b

3

1 Junction 7/8 Northbound roadworks between 9:30 p.m. and 5.30 a.m.
2 Junction 7 Northbound entry slip road wil be closed for roadworks between 9.30 p.m. and 5.30 a.m.

4

1 30 minutes   2 12.10 p.m.
3 To the party – yes, back home – no
4 5.30 a.m.   5 no

B Weather information

1

wind on both days

2

Thursday 1   Friday 5

3

1 Thursday   4 Friday
2 Friday   5 Both days
3 Thursday

4

1 temperature   4 wind
2 sun   5 wind
3 rain   6 rain

5

1 possible – 'perhaps the odd'
2 possible – 'with the risk of'
3 probable – 'likely reaching...'
4 probable – 'will be'
5 possible – 'could turn wintry'
6 probable – 'tending to lift'

6

Friday

Unit 11 Guides

A Map reading

1

1 street   2 lane
3 highway   4 expressway

2

Bay – part of a coast where the land curves inwards; Cove – a small bay; Harbour – part of the coast which is partly enclosed by land or strong walls, so that boats can be left there safely.; Point – part of the coast that sticks out into the sea

B A guided walk

1

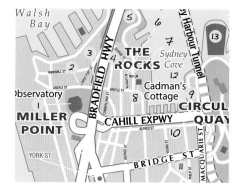

2

1   Museum of Sydney
2   Sydney Harbour Bridge
3   Rocks Discovery Museum
4   Circular Quay
5   Argyle Cut

3

1   a   3   b
2   b   4   b

4

1   take in   3   hang
2   wander   4   detour

Unit 12   Tales of adventure

A   A travel website

1

Annie: snorkelling, shopping, performing, swimming. b
Ela: rainforest tour with abseiling and zip-wiring. b
Charlene: scuba-diving c

2

1   b   4   b
2   a   5   b
3   b

3

1   go   4   opened
2   plucked   5   gave
3   chicken   6   ended

4

1   a   4   d
2   c   5   c
3   a

B   A travel blog

1

c

2

1   b   5   b
2   a   6   b
3   b
4   a

3

1   because it was not a proper desk
2   a soap opera
3   overwhelming
4   his passion
5   They expressed joy at him getting his lines right, even though, in the story, their daughter had just had a car accident

4

1   grimiest
2   struck me as odd
3   wag
4   press (someone) for further details
5   whatsoever
6   lavish
7   blurted out
8   nailed it

5

1   b   3   a
2   b   4   a

6

1   yes   4   no
2   yes   5   no
3   no   6   yes

Unit 13   News reports

A   News reports

1

1   Day and time of tornado: Monday 20ᵗʰ May 2013; 2.46 p.m.

2   Strength and speed of tornado: EF-4, up to 200mph

3   Location (suburb and town): Moore, Oklahoma City

4   Number of fatalities: 24 adults, 7 children
Number of injured people: 140

2

1   Plaza Towers Elementary School, Celestial Acres horse training facility, Warren Theatre, Briarwood Elementary School. Briarwood Elementary suffered the most fatalities.

2   Lando Hite, James Dock, Barbara Garcia. Barbara Garcia was knocked out.

3   That her dog was alive.

3

1	twisting	5	upturned
2	spinning	6	falling
3	flying	7	Trapped
4	bouncing		

4

1	f	3	b	5	a
2	c	4	d	6	e

B   Journalistic styles

1

storm, twister, dark funnel cloud, spinning cloud, wind

2

roar, flatten, lay waste to, crumple, march, churn through, scatter, tear off, knock down, hit, tear through, appear, touch down, wreak havoc on, cross, bear down on, peel

3

1	march	2	roar	3	flatten

4

The Daily Express – there is more use of visual and emotionally strong verbs.

5

1	*The Independent*	3	*The Daily Express*
2	*The Daily Express*	4	*The Independent*

6

Daily Express: It was read by 1,157,000 adults of whom just over 50% were from the professional classes, about half were female and almost 90% were over the age of 35.

Independent: It was read by 443,000 adults, of whom about 75% were from the professional classes, about two thirds were male and 60% were over the age of 35.

Statistics taken from the Media UK website, from a survey conducted in March 2013.

Unit 14   Formal discussion

A   Academic essays

1

a

2

1	radiates	3	re-radiated	5	increase
2	absorb	4	burnt	6	reverse

3

A	4	B	2	C	1	D	3	E	5

4

1	However	4	Moreover
2	Yet	5	Nonetheless
3	also		

B Journal articles

1

no

2

| 1 b | 2 b | 3 a | 4 b |

3

| 1 | as fact | 3 | hedging | 5 | hedging |
| 2 | hedging | 4 | hedging | | |

4

Factors such as…**could all be** boosting vegetation. **(Paragraph 3)**

…this lends **"strong support"** to the idea that CO_2 fertilisation drove the greening. **(Paragraph 5)**

Donohue's findings **make this less certain. (Paragraph 6)**

The extra plant growth **could have** knock-on effects on climate, **(Paragraph 8)**

It will also absorb more CO_2 from the air, **potentially** damping down global warming…. **(Paragraph 8)**

…the future **may be** much greener … than many climate modellers predict. **(Paragraph 9)**

Unit 15 Opinion pieces

A Opinion columns

1

| 1 f | 3 g | 5 h | 7 e |
| 2 a | 4 b | 6 d | 8 c |

2

Answers will vary.

3

c

4

1 Suggested reasons for the results   4
2 Education – a better cure than medication   9
3 The results of the study   3
4 The culture of medication as treatment   8
5 How a study was carried out   2
6 The definition of a key word in this article   5
7 The causes of back pain   6
8 The effects of various back pain treatments   7

5

2

6

| 1 | 3 and 4 | 3 | 6 and 7 |
| 2 | 4 and 5 | 4 | 7 and 8 |

7

| 1 d | 2 b | 3 b | 4 c | 5 a |

8

bed rest

B Vocabulary and style

1

informal

2

1	full-on	4	bloke
2	all the trimmings	5	sticking
3	stuff		

3

Excessive use of brackets, Use of *I, we, they, so* and *but* at beginning of sentences, use of *and so on* (less attention to detail)

4

2

5

Paragraph 3: '44% of the fake acupuncture group improved'
Paragraph 7: 'Proper trial data …'
Paragraph 9: 'In Australia …'

6

Suggested answers:

Health: suffer, treatment, symptom, chronic, fatigue

Research: scale, trial, statistically significant, finding, data

Unit 16   Textbooks

A   Urbanization

1

a

2

1   T   2   F   3   T   4   F

3

1   rural-to-urban migration

2   natural increase   4   industrialization

3   urban sprawl   5   slum

4

graph 3

B   Urban poverty

1

Paragraph 1: b   Paragraph 2: c   Paragraph 4: d

2

Suggested answers:

1   Knocking down old buildings offering substandard facilities and replacing them with new buildings.

2   Improving and regenerating a city area by improving facilities, transport links, employment opportunities, environment etc.

3   Attracting younger, richer, more professional people by improving the standard of housing and other facilities.

3

1   rows of small terraced houses

2   run down

3   tower blocks

4   crime, vandalism and social tension

5   London Docklands

6   young professionals

4

1   Costly; social problems also need addressing

2   Area improved and rejuvenated

3   Alters the character of an area

5

problems within shanty towns	3
solutions to the shanty town problem	4
an example of an improved slum	5
the appearance of shanty towns	2
the location of shanty towns	1

6

1   Rio de Janeiro   3   UK

2   both   4   Rio de Janeiro

7

1   ✓   2   ✗   3   ✓

8

Suggested answers:

1   Rio de Janeiro is the better city, as cities in the UK are not urbanizing, according to the article.

2   n/a

3   The UK is the better choice as the text goes into more detail about the opportunities and problems that residents experience as a result of change.

9

Suggested answer:

1

Rio de Janeiro

Change in shape:

New settlements appearing at marginal areas, e.g. along the peripheries, along rivers, up hillsides.

Urban sprawl up to 50km from city centre

Change in appearance:

New temporary buildings erected made from wood or metal sheeting

Problems associated with urbanization:

crime, violence, drugs, unemployment.

Danger to residents from natural disasters e.g. mudslides and flash floods.

Unit 17 Creative descriptions

A Poetry

1

a

2

1   The Mediterranean Sea, the Island of Capri in the distance

2   Lemon trees

3   *tomato,* a cheese and basil *panini, chinotto*

4   women's voices

5   singing waiters, traffic, voices

6   heat of the kitchen, cool evening

7   taverna, chequered tablecloths

8   lapping water, gondoliers

3

1	verse 1	4	verse 1
2	verse 3	5	verse 3
3	verse 2	6	verses 1 and 4

B Poetic language and devices

1

1	tentative	3	beaten	5	florid
2	hazy	4	obscure		

2

1	the afternoon	4	the evening
2	women's voices	5	the banter of voices
3	*vino della casa*	6	espresso

3

1 ✓   2 ✗   3 ✓   4 ✗

4

There are over 15 examples of this pattern. They include:

the bitter flavour of, the hazy outline of, the lattice of, a complexity of, the rich ruby colours of

Unit 18 Interests and hobbies

A Tips from forums

1

1   computer gaming   3   drawing

2   playing slide guitar

2

The boss is best defeated from a distance.

A high contrast image will appear more three-dimensional.

3

Suggested answer:

Hobby: Gaming

Useful verbs:

loot, disable, wield, ignite, lob

Useful nouns:

dungeon, treasure, medical pack, hit points, trap level, thief, boss, mace, combat, fireball, tinderbox, kindling, torch

Useful adjectives:

nasty, slow, tough

Hobby: Guitar

Useful verbs:

slide, glide, create

Useful nouns:

slide effect, tone, tube, strings, fret, pitch, intonation, tone

Useful adjectives:

mellow

Hobby: Drawing

Useful verbs:

translate, create, identify, cast, squint, eliminate, accentuate, produce, utilize

Useful nouns:

values, media, graphite, charcoal, shading, illusion, third dimension, surface, highlights, range, contrast

Useful adjectives:

two dimensional, extreme, striking, dynamic, flat

B An account

1

enjoyable

2

Paragraph 1: Experiment with simple tools

Paragraph 2: Create your characters

Paragraph 3: Use forums to get ideas

Paragraph 4: Show the world your work

3

1 a   2 b   3 c

4

1 b   2 a   3 b

Unit 19   Humour

A   Cartoons

1

1 d   2 b   3 c   4 e   5 a

B   Puns

1

1 tank   3 balance

2 reception   4 ground

2

1 wave – i) to make a gesture to greet someone ii) the raised part of water which moves across the sea

2 flexible – i) (of a schedule) able to be changed easily ii) (of your body) able to bend easily

3 soft – i) not alcoholic ii) not hard

4 thinner – i) less fat ii) a chemical which removes paint

3

4: to knock sb down

5: on the market

4

1 'ahead' sounds like 'a head'

2 'antifreeze' sounds like 'auntie freeze'

3 'insane' sounds like 'in Seine'

4 'intense' sounds like 'in tents'

5

1 a   2 d   3 c   4 b

6

2: Doctor, I'm not a tall well

7

1 drop them a line   3 turn that down

2 all the signs were there   4 it clicked

8

1: You'll <u>pick it up</u> as you go along

4: I managed to <u>knock him down</u>

5: How long has your house <u>been on</u> the market?

Unit 20 Inspirational accounts

A An autobiography

1

Year of birth / year of death: 1925 – 1965

Country: America

He was famous as: a spokesman for Black Separatism

Religion: Muslim

2

Illiteracy – in prison

3

1 b	3 c	5 b
2 b	4 c	

4

1 c	3 a	5 d
2 e	4 b	

5

Suggested answers:

Advantages: It increased his vocabulary and his understanding of people, places and events in history. It taught him the correct spelling of words. It improved his handwriting.

Disadvantages: He may not have learnt how to pronounce unfamiliar words correctly, or how to use new words in their correct context.

6

frustrated, envy, uncertainty, proud, fascinated

7

1 a	2 a	3 b	4 a

8

Paragraph 3: disheartened

Paragraph 5: bewildered

Paragraph 6: resolute

Paragraph 9: enthused

B An inspiring account

1

Paragraph 10: c

Paragraph 11: a

Paragraph 12: b

2

1 b	2 b	3 a

3

Suggested answers:

He worked as a minister for Elijah Muhammad. He tried to help black people in America.

4–5

Answers will vary.

ACKNOWLEDGEMENTS

The Publisher and author wish to thank the following rights holders for the use of copyright material:

Unit 1

Page 10: Extracts from www.inspiredbypeople. org/charity-events reproduced by permission of Inspired by People Charity.

Unit 8

Page 38: Warning notices from Boots Paracetamol and Codeine reproduced by permission of Boots

Page 40: Public health leaflet from www.publichealth.hscni.net/sites/default/files/health%20risks%20of%20second%20hand%20smoke.pdf reproduced by permission of the Public Health Agency, Belfast. See references on p127.

Page 42 (2): Extract from www. smokefreehousingon.ca/cms/file/files/sample_warning_letter.pdf reproduced by permission of Heart and Stroke Foundation, BC & Yukon and the Smoke-Free Housing website, Ontario

Page 40 (3): Extract from www6.miami. edu/development-training/Resources/TemplateDisciplinaryLettersExamples.pdf reproduced by permission of the University of Miami

Unit 9

Page 45: Extracts from www.journeylatinamerica. co.uk/Holiday-Types/Original-adventures/Holiday-List/Beautiful-Buenos-Aires,-Incred. aspx?subtab=overviewoa and www. journeylatinamerica.co.uk/Holiday-Types/Originaladventures/Holiday-List/Beautiful-Buenos- Aires,-Incred.aspx?subtab=pdfoa as adapted reproduced by permission of Journey Latin America

Unit 10

Page 48: Extract and images from www. trafficengland.co.uk reproduced under the Open Government Licence

Unit 11

Page 53: Extract from http://travel. nationalgeographic.co.uk/travel/city-guides/sydney-walkingtour-1/ reproduced by permission of National Geographic Society

Unit 12

Pages 58/59: Extract and website banner from www.wanderingearl.com/tales-of-a-bollywood-actor reproduced by permission of Wandering Earl (Baron)

Unit 13

Page 62: Extract from www.express.co.uk/news/world/401291/Mile-wide-tornado-hits-Oklahoma reproduced by permission of The Press Association

Page 63: Extract from www.independent. co.uk/news/world/americas/oklahoma-tornado-the-storm-was-a-monster--even-for-tornado-alley-8626094.html?origin=internalSearch reproduced by permission of Independent Print Limited

Unit 14

Page 68: Extract from www.newscientist.com/article/mg21829204.400-carbon-emissions-helping-to-make-earth-greener.html reproduced by permission of Tribune Media Services International on behalf of the New Scientist

Unit 15

Page 71: Adapted extract from www.badscience. net/2007/09/542 reproduced by permission from United Agents LLP on behalf of Ben Goldacre © Ben Goldacre

Page 50: Extracts from www.metoffice.gov. uk/loutdoor/mountainsafety/brecon/brecon_latest_pressure.html reproduced under the Open Government Licence and by permission of the Met Office

The Publisher also wishes to acknowledge the following sources used for information when writing articles:

Unit 16

Page 74: www.citiesalliance.org/node/2195

Unit 17

Page 81: *Italy in One Day* by Mike Orlock reproduced by permission of the author

Unit 18

Page 86: Extract from www.huffingtonpost. co.uk/2013/01/03/ guide-how-to- makeavideo- game_n_2402280. html reproduced by permission of the Huffington Post

Unit 19

Cartoons from www. viz.co.uk/crapjokes. html reproduced by permission of Fulchester Industries/ Dennis Publishing

Unit 20

Extract from *The Autobiography of Malcolm X* by Malcolm X and Alex Haley reproduced by permission of CMG Worldwide

References for the Public Health factsheet on page 40, reproduced with permission:

1. Report of the Scientific Committee on Tobacco and Health. Department of Health, 1998.

2. Law MR, Morris JK and Wald NJ. Environmental tobacco smoke exposure and ischaemic heart disease: an evaluation of the evidence. BMJ 1997; 315: 973-80.

3. Otsuka R et al. Acute effects of passive smoking on the coronary circulation in healthy young adults. JAMA 2001; 286: 436-441.

4. Bonita R et al. Passive smoking as well as active smoking increases the risk of acute stroke. Tobacco Control 1999; 8: 156-160.

5. Dahms T, Bohlin J and Slavin R. Passive smoking effects on bronchial asthma. Chest 1981; 80: 530-4.

6. BMA Board of Science and Education and the Tobacco Control Resource Centre. Smoking and reproductive life: The impact of smoking on sexual, reproductive and child health. London: BMA, 2004.

7. Scientific Committee on Tobacco and Health (SCOTH). Secondhand smoke: review of evidence since 1998. London: Department of Health, 2004.

8. Office of Tobacco Control press release. International studies confirm health benefits of smoke-free workplace laws. 21 October 2004.

Photo credits

The following images are from Shutterstock.

Cover: miya227; p8: Poznyakov; p12: Daniel M Ernst; p16: Elena Elisseeva, Cienpies Design; p17: hurricanehank, Borja Andreu, Kritchanut; p18: Pasko Maksim, Liusa, Kritchanut, KennyK; p20: Tyler Olson; p26: Cameron Whitman, kaarsten, Robert Kneschke, Alexeev Boris; p27: Zurijeta, racorn, Robert Kneschke; p29: Damiano Poli, Robert Kneschke; p30: MJTH, HSNphotography, Bernard Zajac, Chukcha, Bomshtein, maxpro, ayosphoto; p32: Roman Sakhno; p34: stockyimages; p35: Kelvin Wong, Charactoon design; p36: Kelvin Wong, Evgeny Tomeev, ifong, Vitaly Korovin, John Kasawa, Mike Flippo; p37: Charactoon design; p38: rnl; p39: Aleksandrs Bondars, Sylverarts, Becky Stares, Yes -Royalty Free, Atlaspix; p44: LaiQuocAnh; p45: Mark Schwettmann; p48: Elena Elisseeva, Ermek, Brian A Jackson, Monkey Business Images; p49: s-ts; p50: MC PP, thaikrit; p52: bikeriderlondon; p53: Totajla; p54: Lev Kropotov; p55: Pavel Ilyukhin, Paul Vasarhelyi, Andresr, Andrey Armyagov; p56: EpicStockMedia, leoks, Kozoriz Yuriy, Syda Productions; p59: 0399778584; p62: Martin Haas; p63: RTimages; p64: Vizual Studio; p66: Dr. Morley Read; p70: pkchai; p74: Drazen, cifotart; p76: MARKABOND, george green, soMeth., anyaivanova, Andrew Roland; p78: dominique landau, Jose Miguel Hernandez Leon; p80: mythja; p84: BlueSkyImage, i3alda; p88: wavebreakmedia; p92: Mopic

Every effort has been made to contact the holders of copyright material, but if any copyright holders have been omitted, please contact the Publisher who will make the necessary arrangements at the first opportunity.

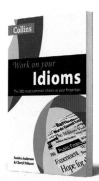
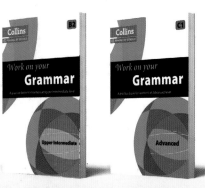